*A Camp Counselor's Manual
for Leaders of
Junior High Youth*

Responsible
with
Creation

Ted R. Witt

Published for the Cooperative Publication Association
John Knox Press
Atlanta

Witt, Ted R   1937-
   Responsible with creation.

   Bibliography: p.
   1. Church camps.   2. Christian education of
adolescents.   I. Title.
BV1650.W57   259   79-87748
ISBN 0-8042-1422-0

Contents

Art by Ruth S. Ensign

Introduction

Welcome to the world of church camping for junior highs. If you are new to this adventure you will no doubt have some surprises. If you are an "old hand," I'm sure that you have come to expect surprises with junior highs! They are as unpredictable as they are fun; they are as responsive as they are exuberant. This manual is intended to help you tap the resources of junior high youth and put them together with the resources of a church camp program so that the resulting mixture is an exciting and growing experience in which the Christian faith is given new meaning.

How you use this manual is important. It is *not* intended to be a minute-by-minute, step-by-step guide to your activities in camp. It will provide you with many specific suggestions, but will require additional work from you to adapt the themes to your specific site, the goal of your camp, and the needs of the individual campers in your group. You cannot pick up this manual the day before the session begins and expect it to be of much help to you. Advance preparation is necessary.

This manual and a companion for elementary campers were authorized by a work group of the Program Committee on Education for Christian Life and Mission of the National Council of Churches of Christ in the U.S.A. Chapter One was written by Tom Malone, author of the elementary manual, *Rejoicing with Creation,* and is part of that manual also. I am indebted to Tom for the fine statement about why the church camp experience is considered to be such a significant part of an individual's Christian education.

Those of you who have been working with junior highs in camping for some time may have the feeling that you have read some of the material previously. I hope so. This manual was initially authorized to be a revision and update of two well-liked and extremely well-done manuals—*Camping in Covenant Community* by Geneva Giese (CLC Press, 1965) and *Camping Together as Christians* by John and Ruth Ensign (John Knox Press,

1958). As I read again these two manuals, I became aware that many sections were still helpful and that to write something new just for the sake of saying it in different words would be a poor use of time. Consequently, and through agreement with the publishers, some sections of the two previously published manuals have been included with only minor editing. This is most evident in the resource section and to a lesser degree in the theme chapter on Community. I am indebted to these authors for the durable quality of their work.

I hope that the contents of this manual will provide you with some of the tools you need to help junior highs experience the joys of church camping and feel the responsibility they have with creation.

I am indebted to the work group for giving me the opportunity to share these ideas with you. I am also grateful to all of those who have assisted me in the task of putting it all together so that you have it in a usable way—to those with whom I have camped over the past twenty years; to the staff members who have tried these ideas; to those who field tested them; to the employers who have agreed to give me the time to write; to Gracie Kirkpatrick, Robert Allen, and Jack MacLeod, who gave valuable suggestions; and to my wife, Velma, who typed the original and each of the revised manuscripts—THANK YOU!

Part I
Purposes and Planning

Chapter One

The Church Camps

It is early June, and school is out for the summer. Books, pencils, and lunch boxes have been put away until next fall. Fred and his best friend are discussing their big plans for the summer months ahead. As we listen in, we learn that Fred's plans include attending a seven-day session at Deerskin, a camp owned and operated by the denomination to which Fred's family belongs.

If we could talk with Fred for a while, we would learn that the decision to attend Deerskin this summer was not completely his own. Fred had first heard about Deerskin from Mr. and Mrs. Taylor, his church school teachers. They had talked about summer camp at Deerskin off and on during the winter months, and one Sunday in the early spring they had asked several of the older students in Fred's class to tell about what they had done at Deerskin the summer before.

Mr. Jones, the pastor at Fred's church, had dropped by Fred's house in early April to bring a brochure describing the program at Deerskin this summer and a registration form. Mr. Jones had talked with Fred and his parents about Deerskin and about what a week at the camp could mean for Fred. On several Sundays since dropping by the house, Mr. Jones had asked Fred whether or not he had decided to go to Deerskin this summer, and he was very excited the Sunday morning that Fred had brought his completed registration form by for the minister to sign.

Fred's parents, too, had given Fred much encouragement. After hearing the director from Deerskin speak at a special congregational supper, they were impressed with the program at Deerskin and realized what a growing experience it could be for Fred. It was probably the gentle but persistent encouragement that he had received from his mom and dad that had finally persuaded Fred to give Deerskin a try this summer.

Why all of this excitement about church camp? Why did Mr. and Mrs.

Taylor, Mr. Jones, and Fred's mom and dad feel that it was so important to encourage Fred to attend a session at Deerskin?

Answering questions such as these will force us to deal with an even more basic question, "Why is the church involved in camping at all?" It is this question which this chapter will attempt to address, because it is extremely important that you understand what it is that the church is about in church camping so that you can do your part to see that these purposes are accomplished in the camp of which you will be a part.

Why Is the Church Involved in Camping?

The basic philosophy which underlies this entire camp leader's manual is that church camping is a part of the church's total program of Christian education. The philosophy implies that the purpose and goals of church camping are the same as the purpose and goals of the Christian education program of the church. Robert Davis, in his administrative manual, *Church Camping,* defines the purpose in this way: ". . . that all persons may respond to God in Jesus Christ, grow in daily fellowship with him, and meet all of life's relationships as children of God."[1] Also implied is that the church camp program should be designed to support, complement, and supplement the other programs of Christian education offered by the church.

But above all, such a philosophy implies that the church camp should provide opportunities and experiences that cannot be carried out elsewhere in the church's Christian education program. It is because the church camp does make possible some unique opportunities for learning about and growing in the faith that camping is considered a valid part of the church's ministry. Specifically, this means that the church camp takes advantage of the two important features that are unique to the camp setting—the resources of God's world and the opportunities afforded by the twenty-four-hour-a-day laboratory experience in living that camp provides.

Much *(maybe too much)* of the church's Christian education program has been centered in the classroom. Church camping moves education out of the classroom and seeks to utilize the resources of the out-of-doors to teach persons about the wonder and vitality of the world and the greatness and majesty of the God who created the world.

Christian educators have long recognized the importance of the teaching environment and the part that the environment plays in teaching and learning. "The room teaches!" has been emphasized time and time again in curriculum materials and in teacher training workshops. In the same way, we can affirm: "The world teaches!" Most people have only scratched the surface of what they can learn from God's world.

Church camp provides a unique opportunity for campers and their leaders to explore and learn from the world about them. The world becomes the classroom where campers are encouraged to see, to taste, to smell, to hear, and to touch so that they might come to appreciate the world a little more and so that they might come to know a little better the great and loving God who created such a magnificent world.

Educators have also affirmed the importance of situational teaching as one of the most significant methods of communicating the faith. Many Christian educators would insist that situational teaching is probably the most effective method of teaching in the church, because in situational teaching the Christian faith is applied immediately to the situations and incidents that occur in the lives of the learners.

In the camp setting, as campers and their leaders live together twenty-four hours a day, many opportunities arise for the mature Christian counselor to share what the faith has to say about life as it is really being lived. Reconciliation becomes not just a biblical or theological concept to be explored in a study session; it becomes real when Susan and Karen are able to talk over their differences with the help of their counselor and to become friends again. Love and acceptance are not just talked about but are expressed in action when the small group reaches out to quiet, shy Sandy and makes him feel important and included. Campers and counselors begin to understand something of the dignity of persons as they realize that their common life together is greatly enhanced when each one uses the gifts and talents that God has given to her or him so that chores and tasks get done. Christian community is felt, not talked about, as the small group wants to linger around the last night's campfire. It is as the alert counselor is able to help campers reflect on their life together that the Christian faith becomes alive and relevant.

Camping does have a place in the overall Christian education program of the church as we begin to see the unique possibilities and potentials of campers and leaders living together in the context of the Christian community in the world God has made. We must do our best to see that these possibilities and potentials are realized.

Why a "Church Camp"?

We have discussed the uniqueness of camping as a part of the total Christian education program of the church and have affirmed the validity of camping as a part of the church's Christian education ministry. It is important that a word be said about the distinction between church camps and camps sponsored by other agencies and groups.

On several occasions the author has heard an admired camp leader affirm that church camping is unique because it has the gospel. That statement is not as simple as it first appears. On first hearing that statement, we tend to understand that what makes the church camp different from other camps is that Bible study and worship are added to the list of daily activities. Nothing could be further from the truth! Simply adding Bible study or worship or other "religious" activities does not make a camp a Christian camp.

Instead, a camp becomes a Christian camp when the gospel begins to influence the whole life and atmosphere of the camp. A camp becomes Christian when the teachings of the Bible and the Christian faith become the foundation upon which the entire camp program is built. A camp becomes Christian when the teachings of the Bible and the Christian faith make a difference in people and their attitudes and behaviors.

In such a camp, Bible study is not something we feel we must do since our camp is Christian, but it is something we want to do because we are Christians. Worship becomes important, not as another activity to include in our already overcrowded schedule, but as a joyous response to the God whom we have come to know in the Bible and through the people and the world about us.

The gospel can make your camp Christian primarily as you and the other leaders who will serve with you are willing to live and communicate the faith that is yours. This is your opportunity and your privilege as a camp leader.

Chapter Two

Characteristics of Junior High Small Group Camping

In Chapter One we indicated what is unique about church camping. Now let us explore some of the characteristics of three elements of camping: Program, Campers, and Leaders.

Program Characteristics

There are three basic assumptions made about program upon which this manual is based:

1) That camp life will be centered around a small group concept.
2) That camp activities will make maximum utilization of the resources available in the outdoors.
3) That small group life will be centered around the desire to create Christian community.

The Small Group

The small group is the basic unit in the junior high camp. It is where it happens, or fails to happen. The small group consists of five or six junior high boys with their counselor and the same number of girls with their counselor. Together, the ten to twelve persons constitute the unit in which most activities occur. In some camps there are few scheduled total camp activities, leaving each small group responsible for planning for the total session. *(Note: Throughout this manual the word "session" is used to denote the full time the campers are on-site at the camp.)* In other camps some total camp activities are planned, such as certain meals, campfires, worship, but still the bulk of planning is left up to each small group. Needless to say, small group camping requires leaders and campers who are capable of handling such responsibility and who have sufficient skills to operate in an environment of freedom.

RESPONSIBLE WITH CREATION

Using the Outdoors

The outdoor setting is the most valuable tool that camp leaders have. If they fail to utilize it fully they are doing an injustice to the campers and to church camping.

A church camp should not try to duplicate what is done in a local church, just as a local church should not try to duplicate what is done in a good church camp program. The settings do not have the same characteristics, but each has characteristics that are unique—the camp's unique resource is the outdoor setting which God has created.

It is not fair to transport campers to an outdoor setting and keep them cooped up inside a building. Neither is it good teaching merely to talk "about" subjects that can be "experienced." Thus, the junior high camp program is planned so as to take maximum advantage of the natural setting of the outdoors.

A typical day's schedule based upon this idea might look like this:

	Get up
8:00	Breakfast
	Clean shelters
	Prepare trail lunch
	Exploration hike—Discovery theme
12:00	Lunch...rest time
	End hike at group campsite
	Begin preparing small group campsite
	Waterfront
6:00	Supper
	Campfire—review of today, singing, stories, preview of tomorrow, snacks
	To bed and sharing time

This typical day provides for maximum time spent outdoors; it allows adequate time for the group to move at its own pace; it makes possible many opportunities for the leaders to inject "input" into the group; it allows freedom for the group to change its schedule, if desired; it provides a balance between energetic and quieter activities; it provides the kind of environment in which the campers can make new discoveries about themselves and their world while giving their leaders opportunity to respond to the discoveries.

Creating Christian Community

For some campers, church camp will be the initial opportunity to experience what it means to be part of a Christian community. There is no magic formula by which one can guarantee such an experience—God's Spirit is the key element and cannot be manipulated. The only thing that a leader can do is try to create the kind of environment in the group which encourages Christian community. Although leadership characteristics will be discussed later, it is appropriate to mention here that the most important leader trait which contributes to this environment is warm, cordial, accepting love.

When campers experience Christian community, certain important things happen to the individuals. Among them are:

Campers are valued as a creation of God and helped to understand and appreciate their own worth in relationship to God, their group, and their fellow human beings and the whole of the created order.

Campers develop understanding and acceptance of their role of responsibility as stewards for the world and disciples of Christ.

Campers develop new understanding of Christian teaching and principles through participation in the community.

Campers with varying backgrounds, including those outside the church, are included, welcomed, and made to feel the oneness experienced in the Christian community.

Campers are given the opportunity to express praise of God, to discern God's will, and to make steps toward realizing their full potential as children of God.

Campers are guided by trained, experienced, mature Christian leaders who are sensitive to the needs of the campers.

Campers are given opportunity to participate in varied kinds of worship which contribute to the campers' growth.

Campers are encouraged to reflect creatively upon the activities in which they participate.

Campers are given a new perspective on life through the experience of being away from home in a new, challenging, and accepting environment.

Campers have the opportunity to have a wholesome and happy time.

Campers gain new knowledge, attitudes, skills, and understandings which will be of use to them in the local church, home, and community.

Campers are given opportunity to have a creative and recreative experience in the out-of-doors, and to develop a deeper understanding of God's purposes as discoveries are made about God's work in nature.[2]

Being a Christian community will mean that as campers live, work, play, and study together, they will have opportunity to come to recognize who they are. They may discover more about their relationship to God and one another. They will be free to admit feelings to each other. They will experience judgment and forgiveness. They will experience togetherness as

14

a part of a redemptive fellowship, enabling and strengthening one another. They will become keenly aware that Christian community is not something they can create; rather, it is a gift of God which they come to acknowledge and to which they respond.

Camper Characteristics

The primary reason for a camping program is to have a ministry with persons who are in need of an encounter with God's love and who are in process of growing in their relationship with God and one another. In order to know how best to minister to junior highs, leaders need to have some idea about what makes them unique.

Junior highs are neither children nor adults. They are early or younger adolescents in a stage of transition and rapid change. Physical and personality organization is so shaken that almost all of them are at times distressed. Early adolescents worry about the rapid changes taking place in their bodies and about difficulty controlling behavior. They want to find out who they really are; childhood images of self are no longer true. Recognizing the nature of adolescence will help you to anticipate what junior highs are likely to do and will make less likely your being shocked by what they may say or do. They need your help in setting limits and standards for behavior, but you must offer your help with tact, with a genuine sympathy, and with appreciation of the serious difficulties they often experience.

The extremely rapid, uneven, and disproportionate bodily growth of younger teen-agers often leads to feelings of distress. Many feel they are either too large or too small, too short or too tall. They don't always know what to do with their hands or their feet.

Junior high girls are usually taller than boys their age. Generally girls are about two years ahead of boys in skeletal structure at this time. Most boys and girls of this age are in excellent health. Boys have tremendous appetites but girls may already be weight watchers. Younger teen-agers are maturing sexually. The feeling of uneasiness about this often results in a desire for strict privacy when dressing. They need help in realizing that the physical changes they are experiencing are normal and are according to the plan of God. Variety in physical activity helps release tensions. But it is unwise to push them into competitive sports which may be exhausting and harmful.

By the time they are fourteen, both boys and girls are nearly equal to adults in test intelligence. They have the ability to think abstractly, to discuss general ideas, and to ponder problems. But preoccupation with personal feelings and thoughts will often take precedence over an adolescent's academic pursuits.

Young adolescents are beginning to break away from the parental restraints of childhood. They become secretive and tend to resent being pressured for explanations. They develop a strong loyalty to the group and try to live by the standards their peers expect. Thirteen- and fourteen-year-olds form many friendships, but they tend to be unstable. A girl is increasingly eager to attract boys, but when she is successful she is usually disappointed because boys don't seem to be able to live up to what she expects or demands. Boys usually feel insecure in their relations with girls and are sensitive to ridicule, particularly in front of the girls.

The young adolescent is looking for someone who will listen and is especially seeking adult friends, who are felt to be more sympathetic than parents. Junior highs constantly seek opinions and advice from important adults. They are as greedy and eager for support and guidance as they were in childhood, but often cannot accept them from parents. The leader with a listening ear who enables campers to think things through for themselves while avoiding lecturing, preaching, or moralizing can go a long way toward filling a big need felt by nearly all young adolescents.

As a leader, you are aware of some basic needs of junior highs. As they plan and function within the group they are expressing basic needs to feel wanted by their peers and to feel as if they are contributing to the group. You interpret the time that girls spend hair-rolling or boys spend in teasing one another about girls as signs of interest in the opposite sex. The signs of rebellion point to a felt need to grow in ability to direct their own lives. Notice the subgroups that develop within your small group. The presence of these is a sign that each early adolescent needs to win and hold membership in an intimate group made up of persons of his or her own age and sex. Their "just-us-girls" and "between-us-boys" conversations and questions point to a need to understand their own bodies and develop positive attitudes toward sex. Their comparisons of themselves to others and "everybody-else-does-it" replies show that they want to feel they are normal. Their response to you as an adult and their desire to know your attitudes toward things reveal a need for a clearer picture of adult living and values. Their inquisitiveness and their alternate sensitivity and insensitivity about relationships within the group will make you aware of a need for increasing experience with the world of relationships in which they must live. When you see the joy that can come from active use of mind and body, you quickly underscore meaningful activity as a basic need. You see signs that loyalties are in conflict and that the adolescents have difficulty reconciling them. What they say and do will often betray a keen sense of sin and guilt. These young people need help in becoming articulate about their philosophy of life and the Christian faith.

In addition to knowing about age-group characteristics, each leader should discover as much specific information about individual campers as possible. Studying the camp registration form can give basic information.

In some camps, each camper is required to complete a personal information form and return it to the camp prior to arrival. Such a form is very helpful and could contain a variety of information. Such topics as family, interests, skills, past camping experiences, likes, and dislikes could be included.

Leadership Characteristics

Good leadership is the most important single factor controlling the success of a church camp. To try to make a complete list of characteristics desirable in church camp counselors would conjure up a picture of "Super Counselor" and probably serve merely to frighten good prospects.

Needless to say, church camp counselors should be mature men and women who are willing to give their full time and attention to the campers in their group and who are prepared to be leaders. Of utmost importance is the ability to live and express their faith in natural (not put-on) manner in all daily relationships. The counselor needs to:

—understand the purposes of church camping

—lead campers with enthusiasm

—be able to handle problems with calm wisdom

—be sensitive to the needs and interests of the campers

—be physically durable

—possess sufficient outdoor skills so as to be able to feel comfortable in the natural setting

—agree to attend all training sessions and adequately prepare for the camp

Styles of Leadership

The kind of leadership you and others exercise at camp will do much to create an atmosphere of acceptance and love. There are three basic types of leadership. The *autocratic* leader's bounds are rigid: "This is what we're going to do and this is the way we're going to do it." The *laissez-faire* leader appears to have no bounds and to have abdicated the leader-role. The group may ask, "Where are we supposed to be going?" but the leader does nothing to help them discover the answer. The truly *democratic* leader will enable the group to set its own goals and determine the best way to accomplish them.

There are times when the designated leader must protect the safety of campers with what may seem to be autocratic leadership. Responsibility for leadership is sometimes abdicated by an immature leader who fears any disapproval of the campers. There are ways of enforcing rules without breaking communication with those whom you lead. Rules are not to be broken. The firmness of an adult leader often reinforces a camper who hesitates to do something out of bounds that others are urging. No doubt you have heard a camper assert: "You know I'm not afraid to do it, but you know how Joe *(the leader)* is about that." The rules of the adult are used as justification for refusing to do something the camper also felt was wrong. The camper would have found taking a responsible stand without the support of the leader much more difficult. This sort of undergirding is needed for seventh and eighth graders, who are trying desperately to work out their place in peer groups. But occasions for authoritarian leadership in church camping are few.

Times when the designated leader should be democratic are much more numerous. But being democratic is not easy. Many are essentially authoritarian even when they mean to be democratic. Consider the essential stance taken by the small group leader in the following conversation with a group of nine campers:

Leader: O.K., it's time to plan. Come over here and sit down. I'm open to suggestions.

Tom: What about a trip to Crippled Creek?

Leader: Well, that *is* an idea. Other suggestions?

Barbara: Let's lay out a new nature trail.

Leader: Now *that* is a good idea. What do we need to lay out a trail?

Don: We need saws and sickles and long pants to keep out of the poison oak and brambles.

Tom: How about a trip to Crippled Creek?

Leader: One at a time. What else do we need for the nature trail?

Bob: We could get Bill *(the camp manager)* to go with us and show us some places.

Leader: That's a good idea. He would know the most likely possibilities. What else?

Harry: How about making ice cream and inviting another group over?

Leader: We'd have to think first about that. . . . Sally, aren't you going to say anything?

Sally: Making ice cream's O.K. with me!

Leader: We've already had it. What else do we need to know for our nature trail?

Barbara: Take books on trees and flowers so we can make markers.

Leader:	Fine. Now, shall we go swimming in the morning or afternoon tomorrow?
All:	*(There is a chorus of "Yes!" "You bet!" "Sure!")*
Leader:	When?
All:	In the morning!
Leader:	Swimming in the morning or afternoon?
Joe:	What about Tom's suggestion for a trip to Crippled Creek?
Leader:	We're voting on time for swimming now. Remember, it would be cooler to work on the trail in the morning than in the afternoon. Who wants the afternoon?
Several:	Afternoon.
Leader:	Good! That's settled. Any suggestions for a game we can play now?
Grace:	"Twenty Questions!"
Tom:	*(Leaves the group at this point and starts up the path.)*
Leader:	Where are you going, Tom? We need everyone's help.
Tom:	I'm going to the shower house.
Leader:	O.K. Well, I guess that we're all set now. Barbara, why don't you and Bob and Kathy do some more thinking about whether to have refreshments tomorrow? Whoever suggested "Twenty Questions" can start the game.

Eight of the nine campers took part in the discussion. The group also voted. Tom and Joe had opportunity to express their opinions, as did Harry and Sally. Thus, we identify the elements for democratic procedure: discussion, voting, expression of differing opinions. But a close look at the conversation reveals that it was hardly democratic.

The leader dominated the discussion. He made over half the responses and both subconsciously and consciously rebuffed certain suggestions from group members. Once his reply was, "One at a time. What else do we need for the nature trail?" To Sally's repetition of the suggestion for making ice cream, he reacted, "We've already had it." His third rebuff to certain members of the group was to use the majority as a club: "We're voting...now." It is easy to see what the leader wanted the group to do and how he insisted on having his way.

The results of the kind of leadership reflected in the conversation are suggested by remarks Sally and Harry made to each other as they walked side by side to the next activity:

Sally: I wonder what we'll have for refreshments.
Harry: It doesn't matter. John *(the leader)* will decide.

Autocratic leaders who *think* they are democratic have their opposite in laissez-faire leaders who think they must refrain from offering any suggestions and make the group discover everything for itself. There *are* things which every leader must allow the group to discover. But the small group leader must at times also offer suggestions for activities and actions. Skill in employing *acceptable* ways of offering suggestions and giving direction and a knowledge of what help to offer and when to offer it can be acquired by the sensitive small group leader.

You should view the guidance you offer campers from the perspective of building relationships within the group as well as from the standpoint of meeting physical and social needs. Manipulating a group into doing things is *never* advisable. As you recognize the possible values which may be realized in various suggested activities, you will be able to offer suggestions that build or restore right relationships.

As one group gathered for talk-it-over one evening, its sensitive leader observed that certain members of the group who had been in tension with the rest of the group during the day were seated together. The leader let everybody number off, and quickly started the game of "Rhythm." When the game was finished, members of the hostile subgroup were no longer seated together. Thus they were freed from the physical reinforcement that the original seating arrangement would have afforded. The group was then able to evaluate the day on the basis of the whole group's well-being and feelings. There is a fine line between enabling a group to face its difficulties and trying to manipulate it into better relationships.

Group activities should not be so accented that the individual is lost. Persons must be free to be themselves in their own right. They must at times be allowed to withdraw from the group without condemnation. The Christian community must accept every person as is, without demanding changes. Acceptance enables change to take place. The pace and the life of the group must be flexible enough to allow for individual members to read alone, to look at clouds, or to play a game with a buddy. Subgroupings are natural and need not be destructive. Every cooperative effort need not include the whole group. A group is really not a community if it doesn't respect the individuality of persons and if it has no security as a group except when everybody is doing the same thing at the same time.

While urging "alone" time for campers, let it be stressed that there is never unsupervised time. As a leader, you have responsibility for your campers for the duration of their stay. Even when the campers are doing their "own thing" they are under your supervisory control and are doing it within the boundaries set by you and your group. In a well programmed camp there is no time designated as free time in which campers simply do anything they want. Everything that happens should be carefully planned to help meet the objectives of the camp experience.

You may hope that all the members of the group will have genuine, warm feelings for one another. But you and the group will not have met your objective if any camper's sense of self-worth is not reinforced. Each member of the group needs to come to a better understanding of self—of abilities and needs. You and the group will *succeed* to the extent that in your life with one another at camp you truly become a Christian community.

Although the democratic approach is usually the most desirable, there are some exceptions. For example, there may be times when the group wants to do something that is either against camp rules, exposes the group to undue danger or is totally inconsistent with the purposes of the camp. In such a case the leader is expected to assume the authoritarian role.

There may be situations when the leader, as a program technique, may purposely assume the laissez-faire role. Such a case may be the planning and execution of a group cookout. It may prove to be a unique learning experience for junior highs to have complete control of the activity and be responsible for all of the decision making. The leaders should observe the total process, remaining silent, only stepping in when necessary to protect the health and/or safety of the campers. Such a technique of letting a group do all of its own planning raises the possibility that the cookout may be a gastronomical failure, but don't let that worry you. A good leader is never afraid to let the group "fail," so long as it does not jeopardize the campers' well-being. Some of the most creative and re-creative experiences in camping have happened as a result of a sensitive leader helping a group deal with failure. It is an opportunity to face the reality that there is not a happy ending to every story, but there are lessons to be learned from each experience. If the failure can be traced to an individual, it provides opportunity for the group to practice forgiveness and acceptance. If the failure can be traced to some uncontrollable factor (such as the weather), then it gives opportunity to explore possible ways in which they could have been better prepared. If the group has to go without a meal because the food could not be eaten, then the group may benefit from knowing what it means to go hungry.

Another kind of situation which may arise in a purely democratic setting is one in which a majority is *always* having its way over a minority. In Christian community the majority does not always win. It is generally considered poor group decision-making technique to take a show of hands vote—it runs the risk of alienating persons, and immediately (unless there is unanimous consent) divides the group into factions at odds with each other. It is the purpose of a church camp to bring persons together, not to separate them. A sensitive, wise group leader, when faced with a situation where a group has to make a decision, will give opportunity for each camper to express an opinion, and will seek alternative suggestions or means of compromise. The following conversation may help illustrate the process.

Leader: It appears that six of you want to take the five-mile hike to High Rock and four of you want to take the shorter two-mile hike to the waterfalls. We can't do both. Are there suggestions about ways to solve our problem?

Tom: I've never been to High Rock and I want to go.

Grace: If we go to High Rock, we won't get to swim, and I'm more interested in swimming.

Debbie: Could those that want to go to High Rock go there and those that want to go to the waterfall go there?

Leader: No, we all have to go together, since we need two leaders with each group.

Joe: Is there somewhere else we could go that would satisfy everyone?

Kathy: How many of you have been to the lookout tower? It's about three miles and the view is beautiful.

(None had been.)

Leader: *(After general discussion by group)* Is there any serious objection about us going to the lookout tower? *(Pause)* If not, let's do that.

You will note in this example that the group has found a compromise acceptable to everyone. This is generally a good way to handle a difficult situation. It does away with negative feelings that persons bring to activities which they approach with a less than enthusiastic attitude.

There are times, however, when a compromise is not possible, and the leader is faced with what seems an impossible situation. If this were the case in the example above, a way of handling it would have been for the leader to have said, "Look, the six of you who want to go to High Rock are the same six who got your way yesterday about fishing instead of taking the creek hike. Don't you think it would be fair to let the persons who gave in to you yesterday have their choice of activity today? Is there serious objection to that?"

You will note that in both situations the leader has asked, "Is there serious objection?" If there is, then it must be dealt with, but generally junior highs respond positively to such a process of reaching a consensus. The general attitude achieved in a consensus may be, "We're not doing exactly what I want to do, but I'm willing to do it and will do my best to enjoy it without giving the rest of the group a hard time. Maybe tomorrow I'll get to do what I want to do."

The ability to bring a group to a consensus is an important technique. There will be many times when it will be possible to reach a consensus but futile to try to reach a unanimous choice. A big part of reaching a consensus is helping youth to become sensitive to the needs of other members of the group and to be willing to forego the fulfillment of their own desires in order to help others fulfill theirs. As a leader, you may find it necessary to remind the group that seldom does a person always get exactly what he or she wants.

Your Role in the Group

A knowledge of the following functions in a group will be helpful as you seek to help the group function along the principles of Christian love and concern. Remember that campers may also assume these roles.

These activities help a group work on its task:

Initiating: Helping the group get started by proposing tasks or goals; defining a group problem; suggesting a procedure or idea for solving a problem.

Information or Opinion Seeking: Requesting facts; asking for clarification of statements that have been made; trying to help the group find out what individuals think or feel about what is being discussed; seeking suggestions or ideas.

Clarifying or Elaborating: Interpreting or reflecting ideas and suggestions; clearing up points of confusion; offering examples to help the group imagine how a proposal would work if adopted; distinguishing alternatives or issues before the group.

Setting Standards: Expressing standards for the group to achieve; applying standards in evaluation; measuring accomplishments against goals.

Summarizing: Pulling together related ideas or suggestions; restating suggestions after a group has discussed them; organizing ideas so that the group will know what it has said.

Consensus Checking: Sending up "trial balloons" to see if the group is nearing conclusion; checking to see how much agreement has been reached.

Testing Workability: Applying suggestions to real situations, so that groups can examine the practicality and workability of ideas.

The following activities help maintain or build the morale or spirit of a group:

Encouraging: Being friendly, warm, responsive to others and their contributions, helping others to contribute; listening with interest and concern.

Harmonizing: Attempting to reconcile disagreements; trying to provide common ground for opposing points of view so the group can continue to work; getting people to explore their differences.

Compromising: When one's own idea or status is involved, offering to compromise one's position for sake of goals of the group; admitting error; disciplining oneself in order to maintain group unity.

Gate-Keeping: Trying to make it possible for another member to make a contribution; suggesting procedures for sharing better in the discussion.

Diagnosing: Determining sources of difficulty; seeking appropriate steps to take next.

Relieving Tensions: Draining off negative feelings by jesting or pouring oil on troubled waters; putting situations in a wider context.[3]

Teacher Versus Facilitator

Each camp group leader must make a decision about how the "content" matter of a camp program will be presented. The decision boils down basically to deciding whether to function in the traditional sense of a "teacher" or in the sense of a person who facilitates learning. The former concept brings to mind visions of a classroom setting where the teacher has all the facts and merely shares them with or imposes them upon the learner. The latter concept envisions a person who sets the stage for learning, provides motivation, and directs the process. In the informal setting of a camp, the role of the facilitator is much more appropriate and usually much more effective.

In small group camping, the *total* experience is program. It cannot be said that one aspect of the program is more important than the other, because every moment's activity is an opportunity to help create the kind of atmosphere in which God's love becomes real to a camper.

There will be times when "content" matter is dealt with during scheduled times of study and discussion. The wise leader will do well to encourage the small group to participate in the planning, execution, and scheduling of these times. The resources for this time together will come from Chapters Four, Five, and Six of this book. Even in these scheduled times (whether they be study times, morning watches, vespers, or whatever) the leader does best to serve in a facilitator role rather than as a teacher.

Teachable Moments[4]

The planned times will doubtless add a great deal of effectiveness to any camp program. Of equal importance though are the many opportunities for learning that arise on the spur-of-the-moment for which the leader does not have time for advance preparation. These teachable moments are times when the camper and the situation have joined forces to make all the conditions "right" for learning to occur.

It is a vulnerable time, when the camper's system is in a receptive mood. Attitudes and values are susceptible to creative change. The camper has opened the mind's door and invited someone else to come in and share. The value of the teachable moment resides in the fact that the camper is ready to learn because he or she is asking to be helped. Under these circumstances the most effective and creative learning occurs.

Opportunities for teachable moments come often and in many forms. It may be a camper's comment: "I wonder what made that tree look like that." It may be a point of disagreement within the group: "Everyone else may want to take the high trail, but I don't think we should." It may be the discovery of something never noticed: "I didn't know that about an orb-spider web." It may be the discovery of a new skill: "I did it!" It may be a question that one had never thought to ask—or never had nerve to ask: "Wonder why things have to die." It may be a failure of some kind: "That has got to be the worst cookout meal I've ever tried to eat!" The list of possible teachable moments is limitless and unpredictable.

Because of the unpredictable nature of the teachable moment, it is difficult to teach leaders how to recognize and respond adequately when they arise. The benefits of these moments are limited only by the inability of the leader to use them to maximum advantage. When the teachable moment is missed, the opportunity for related learning is missed. Every teachable moment is an opportunity.

It was a wise person who observed that some persons destroy opportunity, others take advantage of opportunity, and a few persons create opportunity. For the benefit of our camping experiences, it is helpful to substitute the phrase "the teachable moment" for the word "opportunity."

The weapon most often used to kill the excitement of a teachable moment is insensitivity. Often a camp leader simply does not hear or see what a camper is trying to communicate. A question may be raised or the group may be facing an issue which simply escapes the leader's attention. The cause may be simple pre-occupation with other things. At worst, the cause is sheer callousness to what is happening. Nevertheless, in any case, the opportunity is lost.

Sometimes the weapon is insecurity on the part of the leader. An issue may be raised with which the leader is either uncomfortable or unknowledgable. Rather than expose the personal insecurity, the leader chooses to ignore or sidetrack the teachable moment—opportunity destroyed.

Another weapon is misordered priorities. The leader may be more concerned about meeting an agenda than meeting the needs of a camper. This mistake may be observed in a comment such as, "We don't have time to talk now. It's time to go swimming." Opportunity destroyed.

An often used weapon is employed by the camp leader who is overly eager to display knowledge to the impressionable campers. A camper asks a question that opens the door for some creative and probing thinking. The unthinking leader (eager to impress) gives a quick, very factual "answer" which quickly closes the door. Opportunity destroyed.

The tragedy of the lost teachable moment is that it can seldom be revived. The time was "right" and time can seldom be turned back to recover the mood of receptivity present when the teachable moment first came. Any attempt to inject new life into a postponed teachable moment by use of artificial respiration is a failure.

The first step in adding the teachable moment to our educational tool kit is to have the sensitivity to recognize it. The next step is to have the security and competence to deal with it. Using the teachable moment (taking advantage of the opportunity) also takes many forms since it is a direct response to a specific situation. The form depends upon the situation, the leader, the environment and the nature of the issue.

On some occasions the opportunity may be dealt with in a simple, direct, and straightforward way. This is the most often used. It is also the most often misused. Creative thinking is stifled by a direct answer. Camp leaders need to learn to help a group expand thinking powers by assisting them in the discovery of their own answers. A good method is to ask leading questions that require thinking. For example, a group may discover a malformed tree and someone may ask why it became that way. The leader's temptation is to give a direct answer. However, to take maximum advantage of this opportunity, the group leader can ask a series of questions such as:

—Is this the only tree you see shaped like this?

—Are there other trees of this species in the area?

—If so, do they have the same characteristics?

—Do you see in the area any evidence which might indicate the cause?

—Let's brainstorm: What possible causes are there?

—Of all possible causes we've thought about, which is the most likely? Why?

—Could it have been prevented?

—Was it caused by nature, an animal, or a human being?

—In light of what you know about ecology, should the tree be left as is or should it be cut?

26

When such a process is followed, something more important than the answer is taught—the ability to think!

Campers seem to have the ability to ask questions to which leaders do not know the answers. This should not threaten the good leader, but should serve as a greater motivation. A sensitive leader may say in this situation, "I'm not sure what made the tree malformed, but let's see if we can find out." The leader and campers become co-searchers for the truth.

In using the teachable moment, wise leaders will want to turn to the group for suggestions. This is especially true of situations involving differences of opinion, dealing with failure, or discipline problems. In these kinds of opportunities, it is wise to be able to collect and evaluate all available data before coming up with a solution. Campers will often be able to solve their own problems if the leaders are open to their suggestions. Leaders may also discover that the campers' solutions may be superior to their own.

All teachable moments do not necessarily require an "answer." Some may require a question. For example, after a bad cookout, the sensitive leader may simply ask, "Well, what went wrong?"

Sometimes even spoken words are not necessary to respond to a teachable moment. It may require no more than a warm, accepting smile or an encouraging and affirming hug.

A teachable moment is a spontaneous outgrowth of a group or individual experience. The emphasis is on *spontaneous*. Although one cannot anticipate or manufacture teachable moments, an alert leader can help create an environment so accepting and cordial that campers are more likely to open themselves to desirable change. If campers know that they will be accepted and loved under all circumstances; that they will not be laughed at or belittled if they ask questions that are important to them; that their suggestions will be given equal consideration along with all others; that they are secure in the group—then the conditions are right for them to open themselves to possible change. Such self-opening is possible because the individuals have sufficient trust that the group will help and support rather than abuse or tear down. Creating this kind of atmosphere makes it more likely that teachable moment opportunities will come.

An alert camp leader may, without being manipulative, encourage and create some situations in which campers are more likely to create teachable moments. For example, a hike through an area victimized by forest fire will almost certainly cause questions to be raised by the campers. The good leader is constantly seeking situations which stimulate the camper to want to learn.

The ability to use a teachable moment creatively may be the most valuable tool available to a camp leader. The ability can be cultivated. In cultivating this skill each staff member can:

—Learn to listen to what persons are saying.

—Keep eyes and ears open to what is happening in the dynamics of the group.

—Become acquainted with age group characteristics and the types of questions raised by persons of various ages.

—Become familiar with as many camp-related topics as possible.

—Learn to help persons clarify issues that are raised.

—Learn where to locate authoritative information about unfamiliar subjects.

—Learn when to speak and when to remain silent.

Chapter Three

Planning
the Small Group Experience

Camping is a vital part of the Christian education program of a local church. In no way is camping intended to take the place of a local congregation's church school or fellowship; on the contrary, it is consciously planned to complement the program of the local church. A quality camping program is able to reinforce what happens in the home and local church through the use of a unique group of resources and dedicated, skilled Christian leaders.

The Planning Process

In spite of different settings, resources, and immediate objectives, the church camp is ultimately working for the same goal as the local church—that is, to bring an individual into an encounter with God through Christ so that the person accepts God's redeeming love and lives as a child of God. This overall goal is the beginning point of a church camp's reason for being. In fact, this goal is what makes our camping uniquely Christian. Taking into consideration what is hoped for in Christian education, each camp program committee should develop specific goals for its site and definite objectives for each session of camping planned.

Selecting a Goal

Selecting a goal is the single most important task of a program committee. Trying to conduct a camp without a goal is like trying to reach a destination when you don't know where you are going. A goal (consistent with the goal for Christian education) provides the ultimate destination of a camp's program. As an example, one camp sponsor has chosen the following as its overall program goal:

To provide an experience in Christian community in which every camper is given opportunity to

—gain knowledge of
—grow in appreciation for
—develop responsibility for

God's will for the created order, for fellow campers, and for self.

Thus all of the activities and program for each camping session are determined by and evaluated in light of this goal, which is also the ultimate criterion for adoption of specific objectives for the camp's programs.

Setting Objectives

A goal helps us keep focus on our ultimate destination in camping. *Objectives* determine the route by which we arrive at our goal. By setting objectives each camp session can be so carefully planned that leaders have no question about what is hoped for. The adoption of a set of specific objectives provides guidelines that are invaluable in the process of selecting program ingredients for the camp session.

In specifying objectives, several considerations need to be made. Among them are:
1. Goal of camp program
2. Needs/interests of campers
3. Age level characteristics
4. Camper skill levels
5. Available resources (site, people, etc.)
6. Skills of available leaders
7. Time of year
8. Length of session

A partial set of objectives for a specific junior high camp is given below. The list is given simply as an example of what objectives look like.

Each camper attending junior high camp shall have the opportunity to:

1) Participate in three activities designed to help a person feel "at-home" in a camping setting.

2) Participate in planning for and making decisions about the group's activities.

3) Participate in planning and conducting a minimum of three varied kinds of worship experiences.

4) Learn and use the following campcraft skills:

—Erect a shelter for sleeping.
—Tie a tautline, bowline, square knot, and clove hitch.
—Use three different methods for cooking on open fire.
—Pack for an overnight trip.
—Practice proper sanitation on the trail.

5) Participate in at least three discussions relating the small group's life to biblical material on Christian stewardship.

6) Participate in three projects which make a contribution to the appearance of the camp property.

Note the following characteristics about the preceding objectives:

1) They are attainable. They are not "pie-in-the-sky" impossibilities that would require a miracle to achieve. Junior highs are capable of accomplishing the objectives and leaders with average skills should have no trouble in directing the group.

2) The objectives are specific. That is, they give clear direction to the group and its leaders. This quality makes it possible for the objectives to be used as a measuring device by which the effectiveness of a group may be determined at the end of a session. Objectives that are written in more general language do not have this built-in evaluation feature.

3) The objectives were selected on the belief that they would, if met, help bring an individual to the overall goal for the session.

4) The objectives were selected in light of the particular resources available at the site and how those resources could best be used to bring about an encounter between a camper and God's redeeming love.

5) The objectives give direction to the leaders while, at the same time, providing latitude for each group and its leaders to choose activities best suited to the interests and skills within the group. For example, one of the objectives calls for planning and conducting three varied worship experiences. The exact type is not spelled out. That is left up to the group.

A specific set of objectives to be accomplished provides leaders with several valuable tools.

1. They provide a roadmap to guide the group and keep them headed in the right direction so that creative things happen.

2. They provide criteria by which the appropriateness of a specific activity may be determined.

3. They provide a tool for evaluating the effectiveness of a session of camp and the degree to which a camp actually accomplished what it set out to do.

There is yet another step in the objective-setting process. Each small group and the individuals in it should take part in forming some of the objectives. In almost *no* case is it desirable that all decisions be made for a group prior to its arrival. There need to be areas left open so that junior highs can take part in making decisions that affect the group's life during the camp session.

Each camper should know from advance publicity and from the leaders during the opening hours of camp what overall goals and objectives are to be aimed for during the session. When campers arrive, tactful leaders can begin to elicit specific hopes and desires for the session from individual campers. Obviously, campers will often name things they want to do that are impossible. A sensitive leader will, however, carefully point out why the activity is either impossible or totally incompatible with the objectives of the session.

The advantages of small group objective setting should be obvious. It involves the campers in determining the group's activities and gives them "ownership" of the program. That feeling of personal ownership usually creates a much more cooperative spirit among the campers.

Group self-direction is very important to junior highs and especially to the study themes of this book. The third theme is "Free to Choose." If campers arrive at camp to discover that all decisions have already been made for them in their study of "Free to Choose," they will immediately sense the hypocrisy involved.

Determining Resources

Your camp program committee or director will provide you with the goal and major objectives for the camp session in which you will work. In addition, a specific theme will be designated. If you are using this book as your primary resource, the theme will be one of those developed in Chapters Four, Five, and Six.

Having the printed material in this book is only the beginning of the process of accumulating everything you need for the successful completion of a session at camp. One of the first lists you should begin to make is one that enumerates every available resource. This list should include at least the following types:

Printed resources
    Books *(church and secular press)*
    Posters
    Bible *(various translations)*
    Concordance

Audio/visual resources
    Films
    Tapes
    Records

On-site resources
    Lake, creek, trees, stones, sky
    (List every possible resource)

People resources
    My skills
    Co-leader
    Campers
    Persons on site
    People who may visit or are nearby where we can visit

Activity resources
    Stories, songs, games, poems, campcraft skills

The list of possible resources is your "tool box" into which you will reach when you need help in doing a specific job. The more varied your collection of tools, the better the chances are of your being able to meet your objectives.

The resource list never ceases to grow and change. You will need to add to it constantly as you plan for your camping experience.

Planning to Use Resources

After listing the available resources, you are faced with the question, "Now, what do I do with them?" A more helpful way to ask the same question is, "How can I most effectively use the available resources in order to most completely fulfill the objectives of the camp?" You will develop your own best method of answering this important question; however, the following method may prove to be helpful.

Goals and objectives are valuable only if they are translated into concrete actions. In the example given on page 34 are three of the objectives listed earlier in this chapter. By each objective are listed some action possibilities written by a leader. Another column is provided further input by the campers when they arrive.

Objective	Action Possibility by Leader Before Camp	Action Possibility Suggested by Campers
Participate in planning for conducting a minimum of three varied kinds of worship experiences.	1) Sunrise service of thanksgiving 2) Write a litany and share with entire camp at a meal 3) Dramatize a Bible story related to theme	
Participate in three projects that make a contribution to the appearance of the camp property.	1) Put check-dams on trail to chapel 2) Selectively cut weeds on nature trail 3) Plant trees along road	
Learn and use campcraft skills.	1) Cookouts 2) Day hikes 3) Overnight hikes 4) Build small group campsite	

When you get to this point in your planning, you are beginning to answer the question that haunts most camp group leaders—"What am I going to do with those campers for all that time?"

It is better to be over-prepared than under-prepared. For this reason, go overboard when trying to list action possibilities. Consider each objective individually by putting it alongside your resource list. Ask of each resource, "Can this resource help me meet this objective? If so, how?"

When deciding if an activity is possible, you must ask, "Do I have the available resources?" This is where you use your resource list again.

Thus, a resource list will serve two very important functions for you. It will:

1) Serve to give you ideas about action possibilities.
2) Help you decide if specific action possibilities can, in fact, be done.

The next step in planning is to list what special equipment, supplies, or preparation might be needed. This can be illustrated as follows:

Action Possibility	Equipment/Supplies	Preparations
Selectively cut weeds on nature trail. *(30 to 60 minutes)*	Weed cutters Pruning shears Gloves	1) Clear with camp director. 2) Teach how to use tools safely. 3) Teach what to cut and what not to cut.

You will note also that the leader has indicated a possible time range for the activity.

Taking these steps before camp opens provides leaders with a storehouse of possible activities and insures that there will seldom be those awkward moments of asking, "What am I going to do now?"

By the time well-prepared camp leaders arrive at camp they should have in hand a well-equipped "tool box" of possible activities. The following outline may be helpful as you plan for yours.

Keep in mind that this is only an outline. You should use the resources of this manual as well as others to develop many possible activities in each of the categories below. The more you plan, the better prepared you will be; the better prepared you are, the more secure you'll be; the more secure you are, the freer you'll be to enjoy the experience; the more you enjoy camp, the more your campers will enjoy and learn from the experience.

EXPERIENCES I FEEL PREPARED TO LEAD

Experience	Objective this will help fulfill	Equipment/ Supplies	Procedures	Time needed

USEFUL GAMES

Game	When it might be used	Why	Equipment

STORIES I MAY USE

Story	Purpose	When it might be used	What discussion may follow	Source of story

HELPFUL SONGS (List)

WORSHIP POSSIBILITIES

Situations that may lead to worship	How will I proceed	Needed resources

RESPONSIBLE WITH CREATION

IDEAS FOR THOUGHTFUL BEDTIME DEVOTIONS (List)

HELPFUL SCRIPTURES

Scripture	Specific situation in which it might be used	Purpose	How do I proceed so as to involve campers?

THINGS I'D LIKE TO ACCOMPLISH THE FIRST DAY (List)

...SECOND DAY...THROUGH LAST DAY

---

*THINGS I'D LIKE TO HAVE ACCOMPLISHED
BY THE END OF THE SESSION (List)*

---

*AREAS IN WHICH TO INVOLVE THE SMALL GROUP
IN DECISION MAKING (List)*

In summary, the planning process for a session at camp should take you through the following steps.

1. Become thoroughly familiar with camp goals and objectives.
2. Read the theme resource material provided by the camp director.
3. Determine the available resources.
4. Determine, as accurately as possible, the needs, interests, and limitations of the campers.
5. Develop your personal objectives for the camp.
6. Make a list of action possibilities to meet the objectives.
7. Begin a day-to-day schedule of possible activities.

The Planning Team

There are four levels at which decisions are made that affect the camp experience.

1) The overall camp committee will make certain kinds of decisions about policies for the use of the camp, etc. These are made for you and you will need to be aware of them and interpret them to your campers. A part of pre-camp training should be devoted to becoming familiar with all camp policies and procedures.

2) The staff for the session will, with the director, make many decisions about the manner in which things are to be done during the session. Such decisions might include such matters as who will be responsible for grace at meals, kaper details (such as setting tables, cleaning area, etc.), total camp activities, and other matters which pertain to the total camp.

3) You, as a group leader, along with your co-leader, are the third level at which decisions are made. You will decide upon basic guidelines by which your group will operate, the first day's activities, and other matters that have to be decided before the campers arrive. One of the most important decisions you have to make is how much freedom you are going to give the group in making their own decisions.

4) The small group is the fourth level of decision makers. It is impossible to set a general rule to determine the degree of responsibility junior highs should have in making decisions. Expecting too much of them is as poor as asking too little. After you come to know your group, you and your co-leader can decide at what level they can responsibly handle decision making. Don't "baby" them. Stretch their capacity for decision making by giving them tasks that require the development of new ways of handling situations that require a choice. Camp is one of the few places where life is oriented toward the adolescent. Camp is not oriented toward adults, as are most situations in which junior highs find themselves. Thus, they should be given ample opportunity to control their experiences.

It has been suggested that teen-agers are persons who have a father to decide what they're going to do and a mother to do it for them. Sadly, this is too often true. Camp should be a place where junior highs can learn to make decisions after carefully weighing all possible choices, carry through on them, and live with the results.

It may help to consider that campers may be involved in making decisions at various levels while at camp: (1) Maintenance levels—What shall I eat? (2) Program levels—Do I want to hike or prepare a campsite? (3) Personal level—Shall I tell the group how I feel, or not?

As you plan for your group's activities, don't forget that the camp is planned to be primarily a creative experience for junior highs—not for camp group leaders.

Evaluation

Most camp directors will furnish you with a form or a series of questions to ask your campers at the end of the session. These evaluations will cover all aspects of the camper's experience and are invaluable to a program committee when it comes time to plan for the next year.

Having this form does not relieve you of the necessity of frequent "checks" with the group. You may choose to spend time at the conclusion of many of your activities in evaluating their effectiveness. The questions do not have to be elaborate—often it is necessary to ask no more than, "How did things go?" or "What would you do differently if you were going to do it again?" This kind of day-to-day evaluation should tell you a lot about the group, the individual campers, and your effectiveness as a leader.

As indicated earlier, the most effective tools you have for evaluation are your objectives. Use them to determine if, in fact, you did what you said you were going to do.

Remember, often the most significant changes that occur in campers are in the areas of feelings, attitudes, and values. The only way you can be aware of growth in these areas is to be "in-tune" with what is happening in the group. There will be many opportunities when you can have one-to-one time with campers so that you can help them explore their feelings.

Some camps mail an evaluation form to each camper's parents two or three weeks following the close of the camp session, and ask that it be completed and returned to the camp. Topics evaluated include such items as any noticeable changes in the camper's attitudes or behavior, and general attitudes toward the camp experience. Camps using such a procedure report very helpful returns.

A Holistic Approach

Church camping involves a group living in the outdoors under the guidance of Christian leaders twenty-four hours a day for the duration of the camp session. *Everything* that happens during that time is program. There is no such thing as "a" program or "the" program—only PRO-GRAM. Since every experience of the day affords a learning and growing opportunity, guidance materials involve much more than specific "classes" or "quest" periods. *Everything* is program—meals, rest periods, hikes, projects, campfires, etc. An event may not turn out the way you hoped but, nevertheless, it was program. The unplanned experiences are program (and often the most rewarding). Everything that is done either makes a contribution to the objectives or detracts from them. With this in mind, the group leader must be ready to take the total experience into consideration when planning.

Planning from this perspective, one approaches the task trying to see the whole picture rather than just segments of the session. The disadvantage of planning by segments is that one often ends up with a series of possible activities that have no relation to each other as well as no relation to the camp's objectives.

A leader planning holistically may ask, "What games can we play that are fun but that also help develop Christian community?" The leader planning from a segmented point-of-view may merely ask, "What games can I play to fill up those little empty spaces of time?" A segmented planner may say, "When the campers are at the swimming pool (and out of my hair), will be a good time for me to catch up on my sleep." The holistic planner may say, "Sue doesn't seem to have a lot of self-confidence about most things, but I notice she is a good swimmer. How can I use her swimming skills to help build her self-confidence in other areas?"

The holistic leader has all the pieces of a jigsaw puzzle and by the end of the session has put them together in such a way that they make a beautiful picture.

The segmented leader, without knowing it, usually has several pieces from different puzzles and can't seem to discover why things just don't seem to "fall into place."

This manual is written on the assumption that you will approach your task as a small group leader from the holistic point of view. The three theme chapters which follow are not intended to be used as study courses or teaching plans from which you would draw material to "teach"your campers. The chapters are intended simply to be the beginning of your camp "tool box" which you will use to help build a creative, holistic program for the campers. You will doubtless discover that some of the tools included here are not needed for your job. Likewise, you will probably find a need to add many other tools. Naturally, you will use only one of the themes during one particular camp session, not all three.

Use of Biblical Material

Each theme chapter lists for your use some suggested Bible passages as "Biblical Background." You should become very familiar with them. They will provide the foundation upon which much of your group's experience is based. A good Bible commentary will be valuable and almost necessary.

The way you utilize these resources is of utmost importance. Thinking holistically again, Bible study should never be merely added on to all of the "fun" activities in order to justify the camp's existence as a valid church activity. Use of the biblical material should be an integral part of the group's life and experiences. If that happens, then much of the group's life together will be affected by its members' growing understanding of the Scriptures.

If the leader is fully prepared, then many opportunities will arise to use the biblical material in the teachable moments discussed in Chapter Two. On the other hand, one cannot run the risk of having all opportunities for Bible study or interpretation arise spontaneously. Therefore, each theme chapter contains suggestions for using the biblical material in a more pre-planned style.

Most of the suggestions are in the form of discussion starters for use in the group, and they are phrased as questions to make it easier to get a conversation started. A good leader will want to make certain that some of these topics get discussed and not leave it up to chance. Plan for a specific time each day when your group will sit down together with Bibles to read a selected portion of Scripture and to discuss its implications. The discussion starters are precisely that—starters only. A well-led discussion will encourage the campers to raise questions of their own and will lead to growing experiences.

At the conclusion of a discussion, it is a good policy to ask, "If we take seriously this Scripture and what we've said about it, what difference will it make in the way we conduct ourselves at camp, at home, or at school?"

When conducting a discussion, the following suggestions may prove helpful:

Before the Discussion
1. Plan for what you want to have happen.
2. Make a logical sequence of questions, ideas, and activities that will help the group reach those objectives.

3. But do not overplan. Allow for natural development of the discussion.

Beginning the Discussion

1. Introduce the topic and the purpose. In doing so try to relate it to some experience or event in the life of the group.
2. Explain any guidelines you may have about conducting the discussion. *(For example, only one person speaks at a time.)*
3. Make certain that persons have materials needed, such as Bibles, paper, etc.

During the Discussion

1. Try to involve everyone, even if it means directing a comment to a specific camper for a response.
2. Encourage campers to say what they think is important.
3. Do not belittle or laugh at any contribution.
4. Do not argue or pass judgment on any contribution.
5. Discourage interruptions. Allow each to speak, but do not allow anyone to monopolize the discussion.
6. As campers make contributions, rephrase what they say, if necessary. Help them clarify when they have trouble expressing themselves.
7. Encourage participation by asking questions.
8. Encourage campers to discuss practical applications in their own lives.
9. Try to stay on one subject at a time, but do not discourage creative thinking into related areas.
10. Make notes and assure campers that related topics may be dealt with at another time.
11. Do not be a slave to your outline *(or even to your specific objectives)*. The group may open up an area for discussion far more important than the one you have chosen. If that is the case, thank the Holy Spirit for the guidance and take advantage of the teachable moment.

Closing the Discussion

1. Don't feel that you have to answer every question before quitting. In fact, it is wise to end a discussion with some unanswered concerns. It will serve to "prime the pump" for later discussions.
2. Summarize discussion and review some of the practical applications they discovered for their lives.
3. Think ahead to next session and give some hints about what to expect...or make some assignments.

Notes

1. Robert P. Davis, *Church Camping* (Richmond, Va.: John Knox Press, 1969), p. 12.

2. Ted R. Witt, *Toward Excellence in Church Camping* (Nashville: Discipleship Resources, 1974), p. 6.

3. The preceding categories are based on Benne, K. and Sheats, P., "Functional Roles of Group Members," *Journal of Social Issues,* 2, 1948, pp. 42–47.

4. Material which follows is adapted from an article by this author published in *Camping* magazine, February 1978 (American Camping Association, Martinsville, Ind.).

The theme chapters are not intended to be study courses or teaching plans. Before reading these chapters please review "A Holistic Approach" and "Use of Biblical Material" in Chapter Three, pages 40-41.

Part II
Themes

Chapter Four

Theme 1: **Being in Community**

Purposes of a Christian Community Theme

Small group living in camp provides the church with an ideal situation in which to develop genuine Christian community. In this new situation among new friends and guided by mature Christian leaders, junior highs have the opportunity to give their best to the group and to put into practice the Christian concepts and attitudes they have discussed or only vaguely experienced in their home-church environment.

This is not to say, however, that Christian community will automatically develop in small group camping. A demanding counselor who is uncooperative or selfish may hamper the group's feeling of community. By providing a climate for a transforming experience, mature Christian leaders can encourage growth in the lives of the campers. As campers and counselors together struggle for answers to difficult questions, there often comes the meaningful experience of a redeeming Christian fellowship.

When we seek to create in camp a foretaste of Christian community we begin with the small group in its everyday camping activities. We cannot effectively teach the meaning of Christian community by sitting down in a group to study it. That is an imitation experience, superficial and inadequate. We experience Christian community by giving ourselves in the happy fellowship of a group busily working together preparing a cookout supper after having resolved in a Christian way the conflicts of personalities that flared up among us, a group seeking to be aware of God at work in us and in our surroundings. In such a group, discussions around the embers of the campfire will deepen our perceptions of the work of the Spirit and strengthen our bonds of love toward one another.

By utilizing the camp activities that naturally appeal to junior highs—exploring, building a home of their own in the woods, cooking out, sleeping out, and many others—capable counselors will find opportunities to help the group discover itself as a group and to build fellowship and understanding among its individual members. In such a group, periods of wor-

RESPONSIBLE WITH CREATION

ship and prayer become vital, moments of failure become springboards for spiritual strengthening, and the Bible becomes the Word of God speaking to their lives *now*. The small group that develops an authentic Christian group consciousness is also the group that desires to reach out to share in the larger camp fellowship and beyond. One of the miracles of Christian love and fellowship is that those who experience them want to share their love and fellowship with others in an expanding circle.

Thus, we seek to create out of the fabric of daily camp life a Christian fellowship that will be a living witness to a real and vibrant love, drawing all whom it touches into a deeper fellowship with Christ. Let us consider three specific goals toward which we may work in this theme.

1. To provide an experience in Christian community.
2. To help campers recognize characteristics of Christian community and to assume their responsibility as a part of it.
3. To help campers discover ways in which they can be a part of Christian community in all of their daily activities.

Biblical Background

Helpful Scriptures

1 Corinthians 12:31—14:1—Discourse on Love

Set your hearts, then, on the more important gifts. Best of all, however, is the following way.

I may be able to speak the languages of men and even of angels, but if I have no love, my speech is no more than a noisy gong or a clanging bell. I may have the gift of inspired preaching; I may have all knowledge and understand all secrets; I may have all the faith needed to move mountains—but if I have no love, I am nothing. I may give away everything I have, and even give up my body to be burned—but if I have no love, this does me no good.

Love is patient and kind; it is not jealous or conceited or proud; love is not ill-mannered or selfish or irritable; love does not keep a record of wrongs; love is not happy with evil, but is happy with the truth. Love never gives up; and its faith, hope, and patience never fail.

Love is eternal. There are inspired messages, but they are temporary; there are gifts of speaking. . .but they will cease; there is knowledge, but it will pass. For our gifts of knowledge and of inspired messages are only partial; but when what is perfect comes, then what is partial will disappear.

When I was a child, my speech, feelings, and thinking were all those of a child; now that I am a man, I have no more use for childish ways. What we see now is like the dim image in a mirror; then we shall see face-to-face. What I know now is only partial; then it will be complete—as complete as God's knowledge of me.

Meanwhile these three remain: faith, hope, and love; and the greatest of these is love.

It is love, then, that you should strive for. *(TEV)*

Acts 4:32-37—The First Christian Community

The whole body of believers was united in heart and soul. Not a man of them claimed any of his possessions as his own, but everything was held in common, while the apostles bore witness with great power to the resurrection of the Lord Jesus. They were all held in high esteem; for they had never a needy person among them, because all who had property in land or houses sold it, brought the proceeds of the sale, and laid the money at the feet of the apostles; it was then distributed to any who stood in need. *(NEB)*

Colossians 3:12-17—Marks of a Christian

Put on then, as God's chosen ones, holy and beloved, compassion, kindness, lowliness, meekness, and patience, forbearing one another and, if one has a complaint against another, forgiving each other; as the Lord has forgiven you, so you also must forgive. And above all these put on love, which binds everything together in perfect harmony. And let the peace of Christ rule in your hearts, to which indeed you were called in the one body. And be thankful. Let the word of Christ dwell in you richly, teach and admonish one another in all wisdom, and sing psalms and hymns and spiritual songs with thankfulness in your hearts to God. And whatever you do, in word or deed, do everything in the name of the Lord Jesus, giving thanks to God the Father through him. *(RSV)*

These biblical passages form the foundation for the camp session. As a leader, you should become thoroughly familiar with them and begin to make your list of ways in which you think they can be utilized during the camp session. You should also begin to list other biblical passages that will be helpful in developing this theme on Christian community.

To provide an experience in Christian community means to be open to God's Spirit becoming part of the life of the group. A camp leader can encourage the growth of Christian community by helping to develop the kind of attitude in the campers which allows God to work more effectively.

The Basis of Christian Community

Since love is the basis of Christian community, it is natural that the familiar section of 1 Corinthians be the highlight of the biblical material for this theme. Junior highs will be able to deal with the distinction in kinds of love—*eros, philia,* and *agape.*

Agape is the word that Paul used in the letter to the church at Corinth. It conveys the idea of a love that expresses itself by helping its object rather than by

48   RESPONSIBLE WITH CREATION

desiring to possess it. It also conveys the idea of not requiring the object to be lovable before loving it. Agape never says, "I'll love you *IF*..." and then places some condition on it. Agape says, "I love and care for you regardless of who you are, what you do, or your opinion of me!" Agape always seeks to benefit the one who is loved—just as God's agape for us always is expressed as a means of making our life more complete.

Philia is the word for social love, the affection between relatives or friends. Philadelphia (the city of brotherly love) takes its name directly from this Greek word that denotes love between brother and sister. "Philanthropia" is a broader expression denoting humanity, kindness, and courtesy.

Eros in classical Greek is the word for sexual love. It is also used to express the upward striving and quest of the human soul toward the supra-sensual and divine. It is a love that is called forth by the worth of its object and that desires to possess and enjoy its object. It is egocentric, seeking the object for its own self-satisfaction. If eros fails to win favorable response, it stops. It is the kind of love that could be summed up in the words "I want you." The word is never used in the New Testament.

Trying to define love has always been a difficult task. Paul, in writing to the church at Corinth, did not attempt to define love. He merely told his readers how it worked. If the camp group is to become a Christian community it will have to take seriously the characteristics which Paul described. Ask the group to list the characteristics which Paul described. Then have them list characteristics of love as they understand it (what love does as well as what love doesn't do). The group may choose then to discuss ways in which these characteristics are evident in their lives, and what human characteristics can cause love to break down. In 1 Corinthians 12:31, Paul states that he will refer his readers to a more excellent way. To what had Paul referred earlier, which is in contrast to Christian love? *(See 1 Cor. 12:1–30.)*

Colossians 3:12–17 speaks of some qualities of a Christian whose life is lived in love. It should help junior highs deal with the characteristics of a Christian. Since individuals help create the climate in which community happens, it is important to help youth be specific about the quality of their own lives and how they contribute to community. For example, if patience is a characteristic of Christian love, have the campers be specific about ways in which their patience or impatience shows and/or affects the group. As the leader, you need to be aware of opportunities that arise in the group which grow out of love or lack of love, and call attention to them.

Ask the campers to make a list of characteristics which they think describe the Christian. After reading the Colossians passage, ask the youth how appropriate they feel the description to be of a Christian. Can they add other characteristics? How accurate is the description of the way in which persons have acted in their small group? Can they discover from reading other sections of Colossians why this was written? *(For example, see 3:1–2, 7–10.)* What difference would it make in our group if we all lived the kind of life described? Can they think of specific instances during camp when the expression of these attitudes encouraged community? Or when failure to express these attitudes caused disharmony in the group? Compare the characteristics of a Christian with those of love. How are they alike and/or different?

Acts 4:32–37 describes some of the qualities of corporate life of the early Christian communities. It is stated that the believers were of one heart and soul. Such oneness in purpose should be the ultimate outcome of any Christian community. The unity of the early Christians was demonstrated by their willingness to sell their possessions and give their money to a common treasury from which needy persons were aided. Such behavior gives us a glimpse of the obligations of being a part of community.

Being a part of a small group at a church camp also carries responsibilities. Have the group deal with these by listing what obligations campers have toward the group of which they are a part, toward individuals in the group, and toward the total camp community. Don't let the discussion stop with the small group. Ask how persons in Christian community have responsibility to other persons as well. A good biblical passage to deal with here is the story of the good Samaritan *(Luke 10:25–37)*. Ask the campers to approach the story from the aspect of the question, "Am I a good neighbor?" as well as, "Who is my neighbor?"

Remember, as you deal with the biblical material, the task is to make the Bible *more* than past history. The Bible and its teachings have to become real in the lives of those it confronts. To talk about the first Christian community or the church at Corinth is good if you want to learn about "them"—but camp leaders cannot be satisfied to stop at that point. They must help junior highs learn about "us" and "our community."

Discussions

Below are listed some other discussion topics which may be helpful as you begin to develop your theme.

1) Can we draw up a set of "rules" by which we order our group's life and thus guarantee an atmosphere of Christian community? What kinds of problems do we encounter when we start trying to make a list of rules? What are the implications of the Great Commandment for the group's life?

2) It has been suggested that it is easier to be a Christian within a Christian community. Why do you think this is so? Have there been experiences at camp that have reinforced this?

3) What are the differences between a Christian community and any other group? Is everything "smooth sailing" in a Christian community? When difficulties arise and a settlement is called for, what advantages does a Christian community have that are not present in other groups? What about our small group? Would you consider it to be a Christian group? Why or why not?

4) What are some ways in which persons make a positive contribution to our group? Can you name ways in which others have made our group a better group?

5) Ask the campers to write a telegram to each of the members of the small group (including the counselors). Provide them with enough paper for the task. No telegram may exceed fifteen words. Each telegram message should begin with the phrase, "I want to thank you for. . . ." The message is to relate to something the camper has done which made a positive contribution to the group or to the person sending the message.

After the telegrams are written, take turns reading the messages to one individual at a time. After the reading is completed, give all telegrams to the receivers.

At the conclusion the leader may elect to close with a series of thoughts about the way that all persons contribute to the group. In addition, you may choose to ask some of the following questions:

—How does it feel when other persons express appreciation for you?
—On the contrary, how does it feel when your contributions are neglected?
—Can you think of times during camp when you could have said "Thank you" and have not?

A Plan for Theme Content Input

Throughout the preceding paragraphs are numerous suggestions for using the biblical material. In addition are several leading questions and discussion starters. Below is a very specific outline of a way to present some of the material on this theme to the campers. It is inserted here merely as an example of how to proceed in developing one portion of the theme content material.

The specific planning for input times with the small group needs to be your responsibility as the counselor, taking into account several variable factors. It is suggested that you develop several plans similar to the one below so that you can adequately cover the content required to meet this portion of the camp's specific objectives. Utilize material in this manual, other resources, your own experiences, and the experiences of your campers.

LOVE IN CHRISTIAN COMMUNITY

I. Introduce the session by explaining to the campers what guidelines you intend to follow during the discussion. *(See pages 41-42 in Chapter Three.)* Ask campers to verbalize a definition of "community." Share a dictionary definition.

II. Have a camper read aloud 1 Corinthians 12:31—14:1. Ask all campers to be looking for ideas that will help in formulating a concept of Christian community.

III. Have an open discussion on the place of love in Christian community.

   A. Campers' ideas

   B. Input from leader on three Greek words for "love," giving examples of different ways in which love is expressed.

   C. Exercise on understanding conditional vs. unconditional love.

   Ask campers

   —To name ways in which we condition love. *(For example, "I'll play the game with you if you'll play by my rules." Or a parent says, "I love you when you're a good child.")*

   —For instances in Jesus' life when he expressed unconditional love. *(For example, "Father, forgive them, for they don't know what they do.")*

   —To discuss the nature of God's love (conditional vs. unconditional) and ways in which God's unconditional love is expressed to us. *(For example: life, Christ event, forgiveness, beauty.)*

IV. Ask campers to paraphrase 1 Corinthians 13:4-7, using language and ideas that are part of their everyday life. Share verbally and discuss the paraphrases, making certain that each has opportunity to share.

V. Create a litany to use in a worship service. Let each camper read his or her paraphrase. Between each one have the entire group respond in unison with a phrase such as "O Lord, enable us to love others as you love us."

VI. Sing "Blest Be the Tie That Binds."

VII. Related or follow-up questions

   A. What responsibilities does each individual have toward helping to establish and maintain an atmosphere of Christian community in our group?

   B. If we took seriously the idea of unconditional love, what changes would it make in the way we act in our group? At home? At school?

Other Resources

All of the campers' experiences are means by which they are given opportunity to grow in their awareness of God's part in their lives. Christian fellowship and community are nurtured and experienced as junior highs explore, work, play, worship, and study together. The following hymns are suggested as possible means through which Christian community can be nurtured. The selections of prose and poetry may be used as input for your own use or there may be opportunity to use them with the campers.

The resources here are especially appropriate to this "community" theme; however, you will find that the resources listed in all three theme chapters are, in some cases, interchangeable. Chapter Seven contains additional resource material that may be used with equal effectiveness in any one of the themes.

Hymns

In Christ There Is No East or West
Blest Be the Tie That Binds
The Church's One Foundation
The Voice of God Is Calling
They Will Know We Are Christians
Happy the Home
We Are God's People
For the Beauty of the Earth
O Master, Let Me Walk with Thee

Some Poetry and Prose

> If I knew you and you knew me:
> If both of us could clearly see,
> And, with an inner light, divine
> The meaning of your heart and mine,
> I'm sure that we should suffer less,
> And clasp our hands in friendliness;
> Our thoughts would pleasantly agree,
> If I knew you and you knew me.
>
> —Author unknown

OUTWITTED

He drew a circle that shut me out—
Heretic, rebel, a thing to flout.
But Love and I had the wit to win:
We drew a circle that took him in!

—Edwin Markham

NO MAN IS AN ISLAND

No man is an island, entire of its self;
Every man is a piece of the Continent—
A part of the main:
If a clod be washed away by the sea,
Europe is the lesser,
As well as if a Promontory were;
Any man's death diminishes me,
Because I am involved in mankind.
And therefore never send to know
     for whom the bell tolls;
It tolls for thee.

—John Donne

NOTE TO MY NEIGHBOR[1]

We might as well give up the fiction
That we can argue any view.
For what in me is pure Conviction
Is simple Prejudice in you.

—Phyllis McGinley

CHRISTIAN FELLOWSHIP

As we work...we shall begin to experience true Christian fellowship, the fellowship of the Holy Spirit, which I understand to be the fellowship of people who have the courage to live together as persons rather than to relate themselves to each other through their ideas and preconceptions. Christian fellowship is living with and for one another responsibly, that is, in love. "If any one says, 'I love God,' and hates his brother, he is a liar" (1 John 4:10). And, "He who abides in love abides in God, and God abides in him" (1 John 4:16). If we would find God, therefore, and learn the meaning of life and love, we must live in the world by giving ourselves to one another responsibly. It is for this that the church exists. The church does not exist to

RESPONSIBLE WITH CREATION

save, build up, and adorn itself. Nor does it exist to protect or defend God. The mission of the church is to participate in the reconciling dialogue between God and [humanity]. Here is the source of the true life of the world.... Without this, everything, including worship, is false and idolatrous.[2]

THE SIX M'S OF LOVE

The Message of Love. Because God is love, we are loved. In loving us God does more than tell us about love—the very nature of God and love is disclosed to us. God is eternally love. The message of love can be summed up in two words: Jesus Christ.

The Mandate of Love. Love one another. This is God's directive. It is our duty, the indicated response to the love of God. Jesus, as incarnate love, came to show us how to put the mandate in practice.

The Meaning of Love. Agape is demanding. It demands undivided allegiance to Christ. It is lived out in covenant, a voluntary service into which we put ourselves when we give full allegiance. We are enabled to do this by the prior love of God. "We love because God first loved us" (1 John 4:19, TEV). What we know of the meaning of love we know because of God's self-revelation. God's love for us is spontaneous and we can do nothing to earn it or to make ourselves worthy of it; yet, we are loved.

The Modes of Love. Self, others, and God. "Love thy neighbor as thyself." A self must recognize that it is worthwhile; but if the self loves only itself, it destroys itself. We can love another person from an "eros point of view," thinking only of the now; or from the "agape point of view," thinking of the future, looking ahead and seeing what the person may become. But how can we show our love for God? God is not in need, as was the injured man in the parable of the Good Samaritan. But Christ identifies himself with each person in trouble, whom we must love *as God loves him or her* (see Matthew 25:31–46). The love with which we love is actually God's love poured into us and overflowing into the lives of others.

The Measure of Love. We can't measure our response, our love, by asking, "How am I doing?" We can only look to Jesus as the measure of God's love. In fact, it is only when we look to Jesus that we have a motive for agape.

The Medium of Love. The medium of love is life itself. As the atmosphere is the medium through which light travels, so life is the medium of love. Life is what delivers love, what refuses it, what pushes it around. God loves. Do we?[3]

Chapter Five

Theme 2: **Putting It Back Together**

Purposes of a "Putting It Back Together" Theme

The tragedy of human existence is the degree to which we seem to be continually "at odds" with God, other persons, our world, and our own best selves. If dwelt upon excessively, the fact of our separations can drive up to the depths of despair where there seems to be no hope.

On the other hand, the "Hallelujah Chorus" of human existance is the fact that God has acted and provided the means by which we can become "at one" with God, others, the world, and self! This is the heart of the Christian faith— "...God was in Christ reconciling the world to himself..." *(2 Cor. 5:19).*

Reconciliation is the heart of this theme—the healing and strengthening of good relationships. In the setting of the camp life, untold opportunities exist to help campers learn about and experience being "at one" with God, others, the world, and their own best selves.

Junior highs are beginning to question many of the childhood beliefs which they have accumulated from family, church, and society. Many of these beliefs deal with the area of relationship. Junior highs need to have the opportunity to think about and experiment with alternative ways of relating to God, others, the world, and themselves.

"When I was a child, my speech, feelings, and thinking were all those of a child; now that I am a man, I have no more use for childish ways." *(1 Cor. 13:11,* TEV)

Junior highs are trying to make this transition, and you as a camp leader can play an important role. You can help campers rethink their childhood views of God and begin to see God as the loving God of mercy who places demands upon them; who loves us so much that "He gave his only Son," but whose Son reminded us that we cannot serve two masters; whose gift of Jesus has made it possible for us to know God and to live responsibly as God's servants. You can help youth (through your example) realize that God's love is unconditional and that forgiveness is never-ending. You can help junior highs experience the "at-one-ment" that comes when a life is unconditionally given to God.

The interpersonal relationships that exist in a small group at camp are a living experiment in separation and reconciliation. One of the first tasks of the group leader is to try to create a cohesive group out of the several individual campers. The campers may be total strangers; there may be a pre-formed clique; there may be persons from varied backgrounds toward which some may have prejudices. It is impossible to predict what impediments to harmony will exist in your group other than to say that there will be some.

During the session there will be times when the group members are at odds with each other—boys may gang against girls, first-time campers against old-timers, group members against an individual who is different (counselor's pet, snob, know-it-all, lazy, or difficult to get along with). There will be times when some group members will be alienated from the rest of the group because of their failures—they burned the stew or forgot to bring the matches or caused the group to lose a contest to another group.

These differences in the group may be viewed as problems; however, the well-prepared leader looks upon them as opportunities to deal with broken or strained relationships in light of the Christian message of reconciling love.

The camp setting also provides an unexcelled opportunity to help junior highs think about and develop new ways of relating to the created world. Junior highs need to begin to grasp the idea that the world and humanity are not at odds with each other, but that they are partners. There are many examples of ways in which our misuse and abuse of the world's resources have proven to be of very short term advantage and that the long term consequences of our actions have rather disastrous effects. Humanity can no longer afford to be in the role of nature's conqueror. We must begin to see the interdependence of humanity and nature. The camp setting also provides an excellent place where campers can begin to learn ways in which they can help nature recover from some of our former mistakes. Through conservation projects this can happen. Such projects, available in most campsites, can be a good addition to program. To be reconciled with the world means that we accept our place as ones who co-operate with the world of nature in exercising tender loving care for the eco-systems which support our life.

Helping junior highs have good, positive feelings about themselves is another opportunity at church camp. Junior highs are trying to answer the question, "Who am I?" and unfortunately they too often find themselves in situations where it seems to be the obvious conclusion that they are "nobody." As a result of a camping experience, it would be hoped that every camper could affirm, "I am somebody. God loves me; other people love me; the world loves and sustains me; and I love me!"

The basis for our love is the ultimate love which God has shared with us in Jesus. As individuals come to know, feel, and act upon the love that has been given to them, they are able to give love to others and self. This brings us back again to a recognition that living within the fold of God's reconciling love makes it possible for us to express love.

As a leader of junior high campers, you need to be keenly aware of your role in helping youth to develop positive feelings about themselves. Campers hold their leaders in high regard and respect judgments made by a counselor. You should be generous with your compliments *(but make sure they are deserved)* and lovingly tactful with your criticisms. Let your campers know that you appreciate them and that you think they are of worth. With those campers who seem to have difficulty accomplishing the tasks expected of them, spend extra time. Without being manipulative, make certain that each of your campers has the opportunity to excel at something during the camp session. Also make certain that campers are appropriately recognized when they do excel.

Overall, this theme presents the camp leader with a big task. You are called upon not only to discuss reconciliation, but to live it and help to bring it about in your group. With this in mind let us consider the following purpose for this theme:

> To provide opportunity for campers to know about and experience reconciliation and "at-one-ment" with God, other persons, the world, and themselves.

Biblical Background

Helpful Scriptures

Luke 15:11–32—Prodigal Son (God, self, others)

> Jesus went on to say, "There was once a man who had two sons. The younger one said to his father, 'Father, give me my share of the property now.' So the man divided the property between his two sons. After a few days the younger son sold his part of the property and left home with the money. He went to a country far away, where he wasted his money in reckless living. He spent everything he had. Then a severe famine spread over that country, and he was left without a thing. So he went to work for one of the citizens of that country, who sent him out to his farm to take care of the pigs. He wished he could fill himself with the bean pods the pigs ate, but no one gave him anything to eat. At last he came to his senses and said, 'All my father's hired workers have more than they can eat, and here I am about to starve! I will get up and go to my father and say, "Father, I have sinned against God and against you. I am no longer fit to be called your son; treat me as one of your hired workers."' So he got up and started back to his father.

"He was still a long way from home when his father saw him; his heart was filled with pity and he ran, threw his arms around his son, and kissed him. 'Father,' the son said, 'I have sinned against God and against you. I am no longer fit to be called your son.' But the father called to his servants. 'Hurry!' he said. 'Bring the best robe and put it on him. Put a ring on his finger and shoes on his feet. Then go and get the prize calf and kill it, and let us celebrate with a feast! For this son of mine was dead, but now he is alive; he was lost, but now he has been found.' And so the feasting began.

"In the meantime, the older son was out in the field. On his way back, when he came close to the house, he heard the music and dancing. So he called one of the servants and asked him, 'What's going on?' 'Your brother came back home,' the servant answered, 'and your father has killed the prize calf, because he got him back safe and sound.' The older brother was so angry that he would not go into the house; so his father came out and begged him to come in. But he spoke back to his father, 'Look, all these years I have worked for you like a slave, and I have never disobeyed your orders. What have you given me? Not even a goat for me to have a feast with my friends! But this son of yours wasted all your property on prostitutes, and when he comes back home you kill the prize calf for him!' 'My son,' the father answered, 'you are always here with me and everything I have is yours. But we had to celebrate and be happy, because your brother was dead, but now he is alive; he was lost, but now he has been found.'" *(TEV)*

2 Corinthians 5:18-21—"Be reconciled to God." (God)

All this is from God, who through Christ reconciled us to himself and gave us the ministry of reconciliation; that is, God was in Christ reconciling the world to himself, not counting their trespasses against them, and entrusting to us the message of reconciliation. So we are ambassadors for Christ, God making his appeal through us. We beseech you on behalf of Christ, be reconciled to God. For our sake he made him to be sin who knew no sin, so that in him we might become the righteousness of God. *(RSV)*

1 John 4:7-8, 11, 19-21—Mending personal relationships (others)

Dear friends, let us love one another, because love comes from God. Whoever loves is a child of God and knows God. Whoever does not love does not know God, for God is love.

Dear friends, if this is how God loved us, then we should love one another.

We love because God first loved us. If someone says he loves God, but hates his brother, he is a liar. For he cannot love God, whom he has not seen, if he does not love his brother, whom he has seen. The command that Christ has given us is this: whoever loves God must love his brother also. *(TEV)*

Genesis 1:27-31—Creation (world)

So God created man in his own image, in the image of God he created him; male and female he created them. And God blessed them, and God said to them,

"Be fruitful and multiply, and fill the earth and subdue it; and have dominion over the fish of the sea and over the birds of the air and over every living thing that moves upon the earth." And God said, "Behold, I have given you every plant yielding seed which is upon the face of all the earth, and every tree with seed in its fruit; you shall have them for food. And to every beast of the earth, and to every bird of the air, and to everything that creeps on the earth, everything that has the breath of life, I have given every green plant for food." And it was so. And God saw everything that he had made, and behold, it was very good. *(RSV)*

Since the golden thread that runs through the entire Bible is one of God seeking to heal a separated world, there is almost unlimited biblical material for the study of reconciliation.

The passages above are representative and should provide a foundation for the four emphases in this theme—putting it back together with God, others, world, and self. It is difficult to separate these four relationships into neat compartments. Our relationships are complex and can seldom be simplified to the point that each one can stand completely isolated from all others. The parable of the prodigal son illustrates this point. The son's problems are not merely with his father or brother, but also with self. These relationships affect one another. It will do well to divide the discussions to simplify treatment, but don't overlook the need to put it all back together.

Reconciliation with God

It was sin that made reconciling work necessary. The Old Testament is the story of the human effort to "bridge the gap." The New Testament is the proclamation of God's successful reconciliation through Jesus the Christ.

Paul, in 2 Corinthians 5:18–21, reminds us that God kept no record of our sin. God forgave sin! The appeal of Paul is to hear the message of reconciliation, respond to it and be reconciled to God. Reconciliation to God is our basic need. Implied is estrangement and separation. Our feelings, thoughts, wills, and actions are not "at one" with God. The fault is ours, not God's. God has acted in Christ.

It would be helpful to ask junior highs to enumerate the ways in which humans separate themselves from God. Are sin and separation the same thing?

In the parable of the prodigal son, let the youth read the story from the standpoint of the father. Then ask them to consider questions such as these:

—Why did the father allow the son to leave home and take his share of the wealth?
—Should the father have made the son stay home or leave without money?

—In this respect how does God, our Father, treat us?

—Why was the father so happy upon the son's return?

It may be good to remind the campers of the story of the shepherd who went looking for the lost, separated sheep and who then rejoiced greatly when the sheep was found. This story is told in Luke 15:4–7.

Furthermore, this would be a good place to begin thinking about how our relationship to God affects all of our relationships. The prodigal son, because of the separation from his father, found himself separated from his closest friends, his family and certainly his own best self.

Upon returning home the prodigal son was given the ring to wear. This was a sign that the son was still an heir, by which the father assured his son that everything was just as before. The past had been forgotten and everything that had separated them had now been overcome. This is true reconciliation. The prodigal faced the reality of his separation, confessed his guilt, and sought to re-enter the family. His father, through love, forgave him and put his life back together.

Reconciliation with Others

The parable of the prodigal son gives us some insight into how our relationships with others are broken. The older brother is the tragic figure in the story. We do not learn from the Scripture whether he later changed his mind and became reconciled to his younger brother. Certainly, for most of us, there have been times when we have identified with the older brother. How many times have we felt that we got "the short end of the stick"? There are so many ways that we can alienate those about us. This would be a good time to list some of those ways (for example: envy, jealousy, chip-on-the-shoulder, etc.). The youth may be ready to discuss some ways in which separation has happened in their small group.

In the discussion, you may choose to ask some specific questions about the prodigal son's older brother, such as:

—Why was the older brother unhappy at the return of his brother?

—Was he justified in this attitude? Why? Why not?

—What might have been the older brother's reaction if he had had the same attitude as his father?

—Can you think of ways in which you have been in the role of older brother?

The fact of separation is well documented in our daily lives. Overcoming the separation is the difficult part.

Referring back to 2 Corinthians 5:18, Paul reminded us that we are given the "ministry of reconciliation." The youth can benefit from a discussion here on ways in which we can act as agents of reconciliation between persons who are separated. It may help to discuss such questions as:

—Are we ever called upon to interfere and serve as reconciler between others?
—How do we intervene without risking the loss of the friendship of both parties?

Some role-playing on these situations may be helpful also. One good role-play situation would be the reconciliation and reunion of Jacob and Esau. Read the story in Genesis 31:1–3, 17–18; 32:3–21; and 33:1–11. If the campers are unfamiliar with the separation, read about that in Genesis 25:28–34; 27:1–45. Act out the story or the reunion following with a discussion. This would be a good place to bring in 1 John 4:7–8, 11, 19–21 and to discuss our love for one another.

Reconciliation with the World

As generally interpreted, the Genesis account of creation places humanity as a ruler over the created world. Biblical scholars have recently taken a new look at this matter and have added a great deal of new understanding. Joseph Sittler, in an address at the National Symposium on the Church Outdoors in October 1973, summed up this issue quite well.

> The first doctrine that must be freshly understood is in Genesis—that humanity is "to have dominion over the fish of the sea, and over the birds of the air, and over the cattle, and over all the earth...." The term "to have dominion over" has been falsely understood as "domination," a kind of political word meaning "to exercise control over"; so this verse has been generally interpreted to mean that superior, arrogant, general-managers, human beings were meant by the Creator to strut around the creation with their hats on—their extracting, refining, fabricating, gargantuanly consuming appetites running at insatiable top speed.
>
> That interpretation belies both the love of God for the infinite variety of the natural world God has made and the meaning of the tenderness with which the Scripture speaks (as in the 104th Psalm)—"the springs that give drink to every beast of the field, the birds...that sing among the branches...the sea, great and wide, which teems with things innumerable, living things both small and great...."
>
> In the Semitic language the verb "to have dominion over" means something quite different from what has been thought when translating from Hebrew into Latin, which was one of the earlier translations of the Bible. The proper translation would be "to exercise tender care for"—almost 180 degrees of shift in meaning. Thus, understanding Genesis in its context, we were ordered so to live with God's other creation, the earth, that we regard it as the object of our guardian-

RESPONSIBLE WITH CREATION

ship. We are to have dominion in the sense of exercising our intelligence to see that its integrity is not abused. We are to honor and respect and use nature as a gift of God.

The second ancient doctrine that must be radically reinterpreted is the doctrine of humanity's independence. That we are independent is a plain lie. We *come* from nature, we *are* by the processes of nature, we *live* in every moment in absolute dependence upon nature. We can live five weeks without food, five days without water, and about five minues without air. We cannot live against nature; we can only live with nature. If, out of ignorance or apathy or aggressiveness, we tear the fabric of which our own life is a part, we destroy ourselves as well as the mighty structure from whose womb we were born, in whose web we have had our unfolding history, and whose support and companionship-in-life is the primal place and ground of our existence.[4]

These insights may be new to junior high campers, but are ones which they need to discuss. Ways of developing these ideas are given in the *Plan for Theme Content Input* which follows.

Reconciliation with Self

Beginning again with the prodigal son, one key phrase is the turning point of the prodigal's life. Various translators say it in different ways:

> "He came to himself...."
> "...He finally came to his senses."

In essence, the writer is trying to tell us that the young man caught a glimpse of himself in his terrible, deprived, separated state and then had a vision of himself as he could be. He resolved to bring what he was into accord with what he could be. He discovered what his own true self could be and, as a result, turned homeward to his father. He knew that only in relationship with his father could he be the person he was intended to be.

Many junior highs are in some respects at the same place as the prodigal. They have very negative feelings about themselves. One of the tasks of any junior high camp counselor is to provide opportunities for the campers to experience positive feelings of self-worth.

Feelings of self-worth in our culture are usually made to be dependent on some form of superior accomplishment or on being better than someone else. Because of the rapidly changing physical, psychological, and emotional nature of junior highs, they often have difficulty being superior. Therefore, they are apt to develop an attitude revealed in the common junior high expression, "I can't do anything right."

Junior highs need to recognize that the correct evaluation of one's "self" is not made from superior achievement as compared to other persons. Rather, it is a recognition of one's uniqueness as an individual who is made, loved, and reconciled by God. Every human being ever created has unique potentials, gifts, and talents which no one else will ever have. One of the important tasks confronting you will be to help campers realize that they are valuable—not because of what they can *do,* but because of what they *are*—children of God!

In this respect you, as a leader, can encourage the youth to be more positive about themselves and help them recognize their good qualities while at the same time pointing them to greater visions of their best selves.

You may elect to ask the youth to make a coat of arms. On a large sheet of paper ask each person to copy the diagram illustrated below. In the areas of the coat of arms, ask them to answer the following questions:

1. What is your greatest personal achievement—the thing about which you are most proud? *(Draw a picture; use no words.)*
2. What three things would you like to have said about you? *(Write or draw.)*
3. What do you do very well? *(Draw.)*
4. What would you do if you could do anything you wanted? *(Draw.)*
5. What about you makes other people the happiest? *(Draw.)*

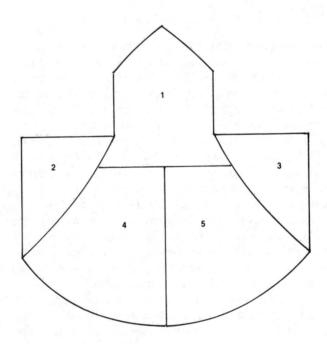

RESPONSIBLE WITH CREATION

Another good activity to help reinforce positive feelings *(especially effective on the last day of camp)* is to have the campers share with the group the quality they like best in each of the other campers.

A Plan for Theme Content Input

Throughout the preceding paragraphs are numerous suggestions for using the biblical material. In addition are several leading questions and discussion starters. Below is a very specific outline of a way to present some of the material on this theme to the campers. It is inserted here merely as an example of how to proceed in developing the theme content.

The specific planning for input times with the small group needs to fall to you, the counselor, taking into account several variable factors. It is suggested that you develop several plans similar to the one below so that you can adequately cover the content required to meet this portion of the camp's specific objectives. Utilize material in this manual, other resources, your own experiences, and the experiences of your campers.

RECONCILIATION WITH THE WORLD

I. Introduce the session by:

    A. Explaining the purposes and hoped for results

    B. Giving any guidelines for activities and discussions

II. Plan for a walk around the camp property in two groups (a counselor in each group). The walk should be two circular ones that bring the groups back to the campsite within twenty to thirty minutes. Ask one group to look for evidences in the natural world where human existence has had negative effects. The other group can look for positive effects.

III. In the total group, discuss the discoveries and begin to explore the interdependence between the world and our existence. Consider using the reading, "Needed—Tender Loving Care" by Harvey Broome. See page 71.

IV. Ask a camper to read Genesis 1:31. Compose a responsive prayer in which each camper names some part of creation, followed each time with, "And God saw what he had made, and it was very good."

V. One of the counselors should be prepared to interpret the biblical phrase "dominion" as explained by Joseph Sittler *(see pp. 62-63)*. Ask for reactions and comments on how this changes the usual meaning.

VI. Select a place on the camp property which shows the effect of human abuse or misuse.

Make plans to heal the broken relationship between human beings and earth by making possible the natural restoration of the abused spot.

VII. Have small groups compose a litany of confession relative to our abuse of the earth.

VIII. Related or follow-up activities

A. Ask each camper to write a letter to the small group from God, expressing their ideas about God's opinion concerning people's stewardship of the earth. Share the letters in the group, discussing them. Ask campers if they think God does care about the earth, and how our relationship to God affects our relationship to the earth.

B. The following exercise developed by Steve Van Matre is a good one to use to begin a discussion of the oneness that we have with the created world.

> Let the natural world engulf you.
>
> Locate a comfortable spot where you can lean back against something. Fold your hands loosely in your lap—slightly cupped—one inside the other. You may want to cross your ankles. Loosen any tight clothing.
>
> Now take two or three deep breaths and as you exhale, let your body relax—settle in.
>
> Become completely motionless.
>
> Don't strain, but try not to move at all. Just freeze. Let the natural world sweep over you.
>
> Within fifteen minutes you should begin to feel as if you're being engulfed. The life of the community takes up where it left off. Squirrels may play around your feet, deer poke inquisitive heads into your clearing, birds alight on your shoes! This is seton-watching, a technique designed after the observation emphasis of the naturalist Ernest Thompson Seton. It is not possible to describe the unitive feeling of wholeness which sweeps over the seton-watcher.
>
> Go out and experience it for yourself.[5]

Other Resources

All of the campers' experiences are means by which they are given opportunity to grow in their awareness of God's part in their lives. Christian fellowship and community are nurtured and experienced as junior highs explore, work, play, worship, and study together. The following activities are suggested as possible means through which Christian community can be nurtured. The selections of prose and poetry may be used as input for your own use, or there may be opportunity to use them with the campers.

The resources below are especially appropriate to the "reconciliation" theme; however, you will find that the resources listed in all three theme chapters are, in some cases, interchangeable. Chapter Seven contains additional resource material that may be used with equal effectiveness with any one of the themes.

Related Scriptures

Genesis 1:26-31—Interdependence of plants, animals, and people.
Deuteronomy 8:1-20—How to live in God's good land.
Psalm 8—Place of human beings in creation.
Psalm 19:1-6—The heavens tell of God's glory.
Psalm 104—God's plan for the world.
Jeremiah 12:10-11—Unconcern for the land.
Matthew 5:43-48—Love your enemies.
Matthew 10:28-31—More value than sparrows.
Matthew 18:19-20—Where two or three are gathered....
Matthew 18:21-22—How often shall I forgive?
Matthew 25:35-41—As you did it to one of the least of these....
Luke 6:27-36—Love your enemies.
Luke 17:3-4—Forgive your brother or sister.
John 3:1-7—You must be born anew.
John 3:16-21—God so loved the world.
John 4:5-15—Jesus and the Samaritan woman.
John 15:12-17—Love one another.
John 17:20-26—Prayer for all to be one.
Acts 26:9-19—A changed life.
Romans 12:14-21—Overcome evil with good.
1 Corinthians 3:16-17—You are God's temple.
1 John 3:11-18—Love in word and deed.
1 John 4:7-21—Whoever loves God loves other people.

Hymns

For the Beauty of the Earth
All Nature's Works His Praise Declare
All Creatures of Our God and King
This Is My Father's World
There's a Wideness in God's Mercy
Fairest Lord Jesus
Love Divine

Morning Has Broken
Amazing Grace
Pass It On
I Would Be True
Be Thou My Vision
Open My Eyes, That I May See

Some Poetry and Prose

ONE WITH ANOTHER

God is love [God] created us...to be persons living in personal relationship with [God] and with one another. Our finiteness means, however,
that to some degree we are and remain strangers to each other, separated
and alone. In addition to all this, we use our freedom to say "no" to God,
who is love and in whose image we were made. Our "no" puts us out of relationship with God and each other so that our separation is made more
desperate by our alienating way of living. And yet we were made for God,
for each other, for love. All [humanity], therefore, is looking, whether they
know it or not, for one who can reunite them with life, with [God] in whom
"we live and move and have our being" (Acts 17:28). [Humanity has]
sought through the ages to bridge the separation, and to achieve reunion,
but [has] succeeded only in showing the sincerity of [its] longing for reconciliation by the quality of [its] repentance.[6]

RESPONSIBLE LOVE

When we think about responsible love, the focus of our attention
naturally turns to our concern for other people. But what we may not
realize is that our ability to establish wholesome relationships with others
depends on the way we feel about ourselves. It is very difficult, if not indeed
impossible, for a person to love others if he or she does not love self. We are
rediscovering that there is profound understanding and realism in the
words of Jesus, "You shall love your neighbor as yourself." His statement
might be paraphrased in this way, "You must love yourself well, and then
see to it that you love your neighbor equally as well."

We may have difficulty accepting this view of love unless we have made
a clear distinction between genuine self-esteem and self-acceptance on the
one hand, and selfishness on the other. Selfish persons who are childish and
immature are not hard to recognize. They are so basically insecure within
themselves that they are driven to demand immediate satisfaction to
bolster inner lack of confidence. They want what they want when they want

it and insist on having their own way. They find it difficult to get along well with other people, and blame others for their own failures and troubles. When one finds persons who are bitter, criticize other people, and say cruel things about friends, one may be sure that here are persons who to some degree hate themselves. In their feelings about other people, they project their contempt for themselves.

Genuine self-love is quite different. When persons know they are being loved and cared about through the growing years in their family home, they are receiving the most precious gift they can be given. Out of the surety that they are loved, children may develop their sense of personal worth and significance. Such development is not so much an achievement as it is a bestowal. Persons discover they are loved, both by their parents and others, because love has been given to them. It is on the basis of this experience that they discover what it is to be loved by God, a discovery which gives them a sense of infinite worth and dignity.[7]

SELF-WORTH: THE PARABLE OF THE EAGLE

A certain man went through a forest seeking any bird of interest he might find. He caught a young eagle, brought it home and put it among his fowls and ducks and turkeys, and gave it chickens' food to eat even though it was an eagle, the king of birds.

Five years later a naturalist came to see him and, after passing through his garden, said: "That bird is an eagle, not a chicken."

"Yes," said its owner, "but I have trained it to be a chicken. Therefore, it is no longer an eagle; it is a chicken, even though it measures fifteen feet from tip to tip of its wings."

"No," said the naturalist, "it is an eagle still. It has the heart of an eagle, and I will make it soar high up to the heavens."

"No," said the owner, "it is a chicken, and it will never fly."

They agreed to test it. The naturalist picked up the eagle, held it up, and said with great intensity: "Eagle, thou art an *eagle:* thou dost belong to the sky and not to this earth; stretch forth thy wings and fly!"

The eagle turned this way and that, and then, looking down, saw the chickens eating their food, and down he jumped.

The owner said: "I told you it was a chicken."

"No," said the naturalist, "it is an eagle. Give it another chance tomorrow."

So the next day he took it to the top of the house and said: "Eagle, thou art an eagle; stretch forth thy wings and fly." But again the eagle, seeing the chickens feeding, jumped down and fed with them.

Then the owner said: "I told you it was a chicken."

"No," asserted the naturalist, "it is an eagle, and it still has the heart of an eagle; only give it one more chance, and I will make it fly tomorrow."

The next morning he rose early and took the eagle outside the city, away from the houses, to the foot of a high mountain. The sun was just rising, gilding the top of the mountain with gold, and every crag was glistening in the joy of that beautiful morning.

He picked up the eagle and said to it: "Eagle, thou art an eagle; thou dost belong to the sky and not to this earth; stretch forth thy wings and fly!"

The eagle looked around and trembled as if new life were coming to it; but it did not fly. The naturalist then made it look straight at the sun. Suddenly it stretched out its wings and, with the screech of an eagle, it mounted higher and higher and never returned. It was an eagle, though it had been kept and tamed as a chicken![8]

YOU ARE ACCEPTED

We cannot transform our lives, unless we allow them to be transformed by that stroke of grace....Grace strikes us when we are in great pain and restlessness. It strikes us when we walk through the dark valley of a meaningless and empty life. It strikes us when we feel that our separation is deeper than usual, because we have violated another life, a life which we loved, or from which we were estranged. It strikes us when our disgust for our own being, our indifference, our weakness, our hostility, and our lack of direction and composure have become intolerable to us. It strikes us when, year after year, the longed-for perfection of life does not appear, when the old compulsions reign within us as they have for decades, when despair destroys all joy and courage. Sometimes at that moment a wave of light breaks into our darkness, and it is as though a voice were saying: "You are accepted. *You are accepted,* accepted by that which is greater than you, and the name of which you do not know. Do not ask for the name now; perhaps you will find it later. Do not try to do anything now; perhaps later you will do much. Do not seek for anything; do not perform anything; do not intend anything. *Simply accept that fact that you are accepted!"* If that happens to us, we experience grace. After such an experience we may not be better than before, and we may not believe more than before. But everything is transformed. In that moment, grace conquers sin, and reconciliation bridges the gulf of estrangement. And nothing is demanded of this experience, no religious or moral or intellectual presupposition, nothing but *acceptance.*[9]

ACCEPTING OURSELVES

And in the light of this grace we perceive the power of grace in our relation to ourselves. We experience moments in which we accept ourselves, because we feel that we have been accepted by that which is greater than we.

RESPONSIBLE WITH CREATION

If only more such moments were given to us! For it is such moments that make us love our life, that make us accept ourselves, not in our goodness and self-complacency, but in our certainty of the eternal meaning of our life. We cannot force ourselves to accept ourselves.... But sometimes it happens that we receive the power to say "yes" to ourselves, that peace enters into us and makes us whole, that self-hate and self-contempt disappear, and that our self is reunited with itself. Then we can say that grace has come upon us.[10]

NEEDED: TENDER LOVING CARE

Wilderness first met civilization in the person of a single woodsman with an ax in his hand. He did it little harm. But another man came in. Rules were set up to define spheres of activity. Another came, and another, and the freedoms of the individual became restricted and later fettered and swamped in law and rules of conduct. Combining the force of its various units, our culture pushed itself like the web of the tent caterpillar across the face of nature. The might and beauty and freedom which inhered in single-handed concourse with nature were overridden. Men became obsessed with the rules of civilization instead of absorbed in the golden intimacies of nature. Men who had never lived on that front line where civilization and nature met, men who were versed in the amenities and laws and mores of society, injected a ruthlessness into the front line. Nature came to be used, disemboweled, ignored, instead of being husbanded, respected, and loved.

Competing cultures began to vie for the right to use the natural world; turmoil and confusion swept the face of the earth. That's where we are now, nervously, ruthlessly protecting our society, our customs, our luxuries, instead of lovingly with the sublime understanding of people of the earth protecting our bit of its domain.[11]

OUTDOOR BAD MANNERS

There's grandeur in the mountain's rugged face,
    Fantastic patterns never shaped by man—
Naught but God himself could do this wondrous thing;
    But who, oh, who left that tomato-can?

I see the rippling stream, cold, clear, and swift,
    Leaping and bounding over crystal rocks—
I stoop to taste its nectar and I see
    Two bottle-tops, a shoe, an old lunch-box.

Why spend a million years to build a world,
    To mold it, shape it, give it tone and punch,
When one poor thoughtless picnicker can spoil
    The whole shebang with what is left from lunch?

—Author unknown

Chapter Six

Theme 3: **Free to Choose**

Purposes of a "Freedom to Choose" Theme

From Adam and Eve to the present the human race has been ultimately concerned with decisions. The most basic fact that seems to distinguish Homo sapiens from other animals is our ability to have some choice about the determination of our future. The fact that we are blessed with freedom to choose also means that we are free to misuse or abuse the freedom. When one examines the general state of affairs in the world today, the inclination is to believe that our choices have most often been poorly made and that we have not learned to use the gift of choice wisely.

The adolescent's dilemma is even more complicated than the adult's. On the one hand, junior highs are reminded that they are "grown-up" and need to begin to make decisions for themselves. Then when they begin to make decisions, they are reminded that they are still children and don't have the "right" to make choices. They are expected to act like adults, but are treated like children. They are usually denied the privilege of a failure.

A junior high camp counselor (who was the mother of four children) approached her camp director one day about the middle of the camp session. She was frustrated with her group's performance and reported this to the director. When asked to explain the difficulty, the counselor commented, "These campers do not know how to make a decision. They just can't decide anything." How typical of junior highs. The important thing though is *why* they do not know how to make decisions. Could it be the fact that few of them have had regular opportunity to make important decisions that affect their lives?

Junior highs are crying for freedom from restraints—restraints from parental control, social mores, religion's rules, and governmental regulations. They are turning from external controls to more internalized controls, and this is precisely the point at which an experience at camp can make such positive contributions.

RESPONSIBLE WITH CREATION

Youth want freedom, but not *total* freedom. They want to be able to try things on their own, but want to maintain the security of a "constant" in their lives. They want something on which they can depend, no matter how much everything else changes. They generally want to be given a very long tether which allows them to roam almost at will, but which is still securely connected at one end so that they can choose to return to more familiar territory.

If all decision making were a choice between two directly opposed alternatives, our lives would be simplified; few such black-white issues exist. Most important decisions require the identification and consideration of many alternatives. Junior highs have seldom developed the skills necessary to handle such complicated problems. In a camp setting, however, the campers have several advantages when it comes to making decisions.

1. Camp life is a much more simple setting. Many of the usually present extraneous factors that serve to complicate what might otherwise be a simple decision are not present at camp.
2. At camp, junior highs help run a world oriented toward youth, not adults.
3. The youth are free from the presence of their parents, who often inhibit their desire to make decisions.
4. Camp provides a safe setting in which youth can "play with" or "try on" new freedoms.
5. The simplified small group camp setting provides the opportunity for junior highs to learn and see how their decisions affect themselves and others.
6. Camp provides the kind of supportive fellowship in which campers are encouraged to make decisions.
7. Camp provides the mature adult guidance (the "constant" spoken of earlier) so needed if youth are going to learn how to make responsible and intelligent decisions.
8. Camp provides the setting of Christian community which inherently provides that one of the considerations in decision making be that of the role of Christian love.
9. The nature of small group camping provides many situations in which built-in decisions are necessary. The decisions are not earth-shattering, but they are basic to the well-being of the group. A well-made decision can be bragged about, while a poor choice can serve as a building stone from which valuable lessons can be learned and upon which future choices be made.

The camp leader needs to be reminded that life at camp is not merely "life-oriented"—it is life, and an important part of the life of the junior high camper. During the session in which you serve some decisions will be made that will change and heavily influence the campers for the rest of their lives. At camp, we are not simply "playing life" (as we used to "play house"). We are "living," and the lives of our campers are at stake.

One of the most valuable gifts that junior high campers can receive from an experience in camp is to become better equipped to make important decisions, taking into consideration the demands of the Christian faith upon their lives.

The hope is that campers will begin to build the kind of value system that will provide them with the input they need to make responsible decisions. We, as leaders, dare not take away their freedom to choose by trying to impose our values upon them. Indeed, it would be futile to try to give them our values. We can't do that; however, we can give guidance, provide influence, and enable the campers to clarify their values so that they begin to evolve their own permanent values.

John H. Westerhoff, III, writing about the book *Values and Teaching*, by Raths, Harmin, and Simon, states the essentials by which persons are enabled to initiate the adoption of their own values.

—First, encourage children to make choices and to make them freely.

—Second, help them discover available alternatives when faced with choices.

—Third, help them weigh alternatives thoroughly, reflecting on the consequences of each.

—Fourth, encourage them to consider what it is they prize and cherish.

—Fifth, give them opportunity to make public affirmation of their choices.

—Sixth, encourage them to act, behave, and live in accordance with their choices.

—Last, help them to examine repeated patterns of behavior in their lives.[12]

With this important task in mind, then, let us consider the following purposes of the theme, "Freedom to Choose":

1. To help campers recognize situations in which decisions need to be made.
2. To assist and encourage the campers in responsible decision making as it affects themselves and their relationships to others, the world, and God.
3. To help campers accept and evaluate the results of their decisions.

RESPONSIBLE WITH CREATION

Biblical Background

Helpful Scriptures:

Genesis 3:1-6

Now the serpent was more subtle than any other wild creature that the Lord God had made. He said to the woman, "Did God say, 'You shall not eat of any tree of the garden'?" And the woman said to the serpent, "We may eat of the fruit of the trees of the garden; but God said, 'You shall not eat of the fruit of the tree which is in the midst of the garden, neither shall you touch it, lest you die.'" But the serpent said to the woman, "You will not die. For God knows that when you eat of it your eyes will be opened, and you will be like God, knowing good and evil." So when the woman saw that the tree was good for food, and that it was a delight to the eyes, and that the tree was to be desired to make one wise, she took of its fruit and ate; and she also gave some to her husband, and he ate. *(RSV)*

Luke 4:1-13

Jesus returned from the Jordan full of the Holy Spirit and was led by the Spirit into the desert, where he was tempted by the Devil for forty days. In all that time he ate nothing, so that he was hungry when it was over.

The Devil said to him, "If you are God's Son, order this stone to turn into bread." But Jesus answered, "The scripture says, 'Man cannot live on bread alone.'"

Then the Devil took him up and showed him in a second all the kingdoms of the world. "I will give you all this power and all this wealth," the Devil told him. "It has all been handed over to me, and I can give it to anyone I choose. All this will be yours, then, if you worship me." Jesus answered, "The scripture says, 'Worship the Lord your God and serve only him!'"

Then the Devil took him to Jerusalem and set him on the highest point of the Temple, and said to him, "If you are God's Son, throw yourself down from here. For the scripture says, 'God will order his angels to take good care of you.' It also says, 'They will hold you up with their hands so that not even your feet will be hurt on the stones.'" But Jesus answered, "The scripture says, 'Do not put the Lord your God to the test.'" When the Devil finished tempting Jesus in every way, he left him for a while. *(TEV)*

Matthew 6:24

No one can serve two masters; for either he will hate the one and love the other, or he will be devoted to the one and despise the other. *(RSV)*

Matthew 19:16-22

Once a man came to Jesus. "Teacher," he asked, "what good thing must I do to receive eternal life?"

"Why do you ask me concerning what is good?" answered Jesus. "There is only One who is good. Keep the commandments if you want to enter life."

"What commandments?" he asked.

Jesus answered, "Do not commit murder; do not commit adultery; do not steal; do not accuse anyone falsely. Respect your father and mother; and love your neighbor as you love yourself."

"I have obeyed all these commandments," the young man replied. "What else do I need to do?"

Jesus said to him, "If you want to be perfect, go and sell all you have and give the money to the poor, and you will have riches in heaven; then come and follow me."

When the young man heard this, he went away sad, because he was very rich. *(TEV)*

When Adam and Eve decided to eat the fruit of the tree of knowledge of good and evil, they made a decision which changed the lives of all who have followed. They had the freedom to choose. They were not puppets on a string to be manipulated at God's whim. They were persons with minds with which to think and the ability to alter the course of their lives.

The Meaning of Freedom

We begin our study with an acknowledgment that we are faced daily with decisions that have to be made. God has created us with freedom to choose, and many of the decisions we face are crucial.

Genesis 3:1–6 describes the temptation and fall of Adam and Eve while Luke 4:1–13 describes the temptation and victory of Jesus. In both of these cases the decisions facing the individuals were ones which determined the nature of their future.

Junior highs, after reading these two passages, can discuss the meaning of freedom. What does it mean to be free? What is the difference between freedom and license? One of the main points in the temptation stories is that Adam and Eve as well as Jesus had the freedom to choose. In Adam and Eve's case, they chose to ignore God's will. In Jesus' case, he chose to obey God's will. Junior high campers need to begin to realize that freedom is a gift from God which carries with it certain responsibilities. Can we ever be truly free? Are there any decisions we make that never affect other persons or our relationship to them? Can we ever be truly independent of others?

Discuss the similarities and differences in the two temptation stories. Do these decisions affect us? If so, how? Upon what basis did Adam and Eve make their decision? What was the basis of Jesus' decisions?

Recognizing temptation and the need for decision is one of the more difficult problems faced by junior highs. Ask the youth to discuss the most important decision they have made in the past year, and to speculate on decisions they may have to face in the coming months.

RESPONSIBLE WITH CREATION

Forced Choices

There are many occasions when we are forced into making a decision. We have no choice except to decide one way or another. Matthew 6:24 reminds us forcefully of this. The choice which Jesus describes is between God and mammon. Many modern translators substitute the word "money" for mammon. The word actually means all facets of worldliness including money, success, and love of possessions. Love of God and love of mammon are mutually exclusive and it is impossible to love both. Even not to decide is to make a choice.

Junior highs are faced with many such choices which they can neither anticipate nor avoid. For example, we are given too much change in a store. What do we do? Or, we observe someone in school cheating. What do we do? Or, we see an automobile accident, but no one knows we saw it. What do we do?

Let the campers think of other situations in which they are forced to make decisions.

Making Decisions

Recognizing that choices need to be made is the first step. Knowing how to make a decision so that it contributes to one's well-being is another problem in itself. Making decisions involves discovering and weighing possible alternatives. Unfortunately, there are no hard and fast rules to guarantee the right choice.

Matthew 19:16–22 tells the story of a man who faced a decision and made the wrong choice. As the campers read the account, make certain that they understand what the young man was asking—that is, for a new command which superseded the old and which would guarantee him eternal life. He was disappointed when Jesus had no new "rule" to follow. Instead, the young man was instructed to sell his belongings, give the money to the poor, and follow Jesus. This was too much for him! Ask the campers what the story tells us about the young man's values, and try to uncover the criteria upon which the decision was based. Did he consider all of the alternatives or their consequences?

A sign of maturity in decision making is to be able to foresee some of the possible long-range consequences of each alternative and to choose upon the basis of that foresight. What possible consequences did the rich young man consider most important?

Another sign of maturity in decision making is being able to "live with" the consequences of the decision once it is made. The only thing we know for sure about the young man is that he decided not to follow Jesus and went away sorrowful. The end of the story is hidden from our view.

As the small group plans for all of its activities, making decisions is an important part of the group's life. There should be opportunity to ask questions about how responsible the group's decisions are.

Remember, you are not trying to give junior highs all the answers. You are seeking to give them guidance so that in the future they will know *how* to make decisions in the light of the demands of God's love in their lives.

A Plan for Theme Content Input

Throughout the preceding paragraphs are numerous suggestions for using the biblical material. In addition are several leading questions and discussion starters. Below is a very specific outline of a way to present some of the material on this theme to the campers. It is inserted here merely as an example of how to proceed in developing the theme content.

The specific planning for input times with the small group needs to fall to you, the counselor, taking into account several variable factors. It is suggested that you develop several plans similar to the one below so that you can adequately cover the content required to meet this portion of the camp's specific objectives. Utilize material in this manual, other resources, your own experiences, and the experiences of your campers.

CONSIDERING AVAILABLE ALTERNATIVES WHEN FACING A DECISION

I. Introduce the session by:

A. Explaining the purposes and hoped-for results.

B. Giving any guidelines for activities and discussions.

II. Play "Either-Or Forced Choice"

This exercise forces campers to make a choice between two alternatives. The counselor asks all campers to stand in a group and then gives directions in the following manner. "Are you more like an oak tree or a palm tree? If you are like an oak go to your left. If you are like a palm go to your right. You have to make a decision—you cannot remain in the center." After everyone has made the decision ask them to talk for no more than two minutes about why they made the choice they did. Then ask someone from each group to share the essence of the conversation.

Bring all back to the center and repeat the process several times with other choices. At the conclusion ask the campers if they had difficulty making a choice and if so, why? If there were occasions when one person stood alone, ask how it felt.

Some suggestions for choices are: summer or winter; stream or ocean; eagle or canary; mountain or valley; rose or daisy; canoe or motorboat; sun or moon. The leader may think of others more appropriate.[13]

III. Introduce ideas from "A Place Called Neutrality" (see page 82). Point out that we constantly face situations that require a decision and that seldom are they a simple "either-or" situation as in our game. Usually there are several alternatives and one of our tasks is to learn to uncover and consider all possible choices.

IV. As an example of how many alternatives we have, ask the group to plan a menu for a group cookout. Take into consideration such factors as food available from kitchen, likes and dislikes of group members, time and cooking equipment available, cost, world hunger, etc. Help group (by asking probing questions) to discover how complex decision making can be. Then lead them to see how much simpler it becomes when we first list all possible alternatives and choose by process of elimination, ultimately selecting the best of the alternatives.

V. Ask group to read Matthew 19:16-22. Ask them to consider the alternatives. Did the young man have more than two? Why did he choose the one he did? Would we have done differently? A role play may be helpful. Ask the group to write and act out two endings to the story—one based on the story as we have it, the other as if he had done what Jesus demanded.

VI. Ask the campers if they can think of situations now in which God places such demands upon persons?

What was Matthew trying to tell us about values and priorities?

VII. For a worship setting, the campers may make a choral reading from the poem, "The Rich Young Ruler" (see page 83). It could be shared with another group.

VIII. Related or Follow-up Activities
   A. Use the hymn, "I Surrender All," as a setting to discuss the nature of the demands placed upon us when we make a commitment to God through Christ.
   B. Go around the group and let each camper complete this sentence, "The decision that I have recently made of which I am most proud is...."

C. Play "Take Shelter."
Your campers are responsible for making a decision that will determine life or death for some other persons. The setting is this: There are ten persons who live at a Human Ecology Commune at which a radioactive accident has occurred. A shelter there will hold only six persons. There will not be room for four of the persons. Your group has thirty minutes to decide which six will go into the shelter. If decision is not made by then, all will die. The ten people are:

1) Nuclear scientist, age 47, whose careless experiments caused the accident
2) His wife, four months pregnant
3) A young female physician, capable but known to be unstable
4) A famous psychologist-author, age 60
5) A television talk show host
6) Professional football player, low IQ
7) High school sophomore, majorette
8) Skilled manual worker, age 40, illiterate
9) A blind orthodox priest, age 70
10) Former presidential assistant, disbarred lawyer, clever, but shifty

Procedure:
—Introduce task and setting.
—Introduce the characters.
—Give campers five minutes (acting alone) to rank all ten persons in order of desirability for survival.
—Give group twenty-five minutes to reach a concensus on the six survivors.

—Follow up:
   a) Did you listen to opinions of others in group?
   b) Were you inclined to change your mind because of group pressures? Logical arguments?
   c) Did anyone's single-mindedness prevent group from making decision on time?
   d) After the group made a decision different from yours, did you think yours was still right?
   e) What made the decisions difficult?
   f) Would a person's status as a Christian or non-Christian affect the decisions?[14]

Other Resources

All of the campers' experiences are means by which they are given opportunity to grow in their awareness of God's part in their lives. Christian fellowship and community are nurtured and experienced as junior highs explore, work, play, worship, and study together. The following activities are suggested as possible means through which Christian community can be nurtured. The selections of prose and poetry may be used as input for your own use or there may be opportunity to use them with the campers.

The resources here are especially appropriate to this "Free to Choose" theme; however, you will find that the resources listed in all three theme chapters are, in some cases, interchangeable. Part III contains additional resource material that may be used with equal effectiveness with any one of the themes.

Other Related Scriptures

Isaiah 6:1–9—Isaiah's call.
Matthew 6:19–21—Where your treasure is....
Matthew 8:19–22—"Follow me."
Matthew 23:23–24—Straining out a gnat and swallowing a camel.
Matthew 26:14–16—Judas' betrayal.
Matthew 26:69–75—Peter's denial.
Mark 8:34–38—What does it profit?
Luke 10:38–42—Mary and Martha.
Luke 12:23–31—Life is more than food.
John 12:42–43—"They loved the praise of men more than the praise of God."
Acts 9:1–31—Paul's conversion.
2 Corinthians 13:5–9—Examine yourselves.

Hymns

Jesus Calls Us
Lord, Speak to Me
Have Thine Own Way, Lord
O Jesus, I Have Promised
Lord, I Want to Be a Christian
I've Found a Friend
Yield Not to Temptation
I Surrender All
Take My Life
The Voice of God Is Calling
"Are Ye Able," Said the Master

A PLACE CALLED NEUTRALITY

I searched for a place called neutrality,
   A place that is in-between,
   A place where I would not have to take sides
      and could stand uncommitted.

I searched for a place called neutrality,
   A place where I wouldn't have to decide
      what is right or wrong or good or bad;
   A place where a decision would be unnecessary
      because nothing really mattered;
      or, if it did, the decision would already be made for me.

I searched for a place called neutrality,
   A place where I could be everything to everyone,
   A place where I could please everyone
      because I could be to everyone exactly what they
         wanted me to be.

I searched for a place called neutrality
      because I was tired of always having someone disagree with me—
         someone discredit me when I tried to stand for something—
      tired of controversy and insecurity;
So I began to search for a place where I could remain
   completely neutral.

I found a place called neutrality,
   A place that is in-between,
   A place where I did not have to take sides,
      and could stand uncommitted,
   A place where I could hide and avoid making a decision,
   A place that was safe from the criticism of others.

But when I found that place, what I saw was strange.

The people that I saw were not really persons.
   They were simply bodies—physical bodies—
      trying to escape the reality of being;
      trying to escape making a decision which would
         affect themselves and others;
      trying to escape committing themselves to anything;
      trying to escape being a person,
         and, in fact, doing a good job of escaping being.

The people that I saw were not really persons,
   They were empty shells who had lost their inner courage
      to stand for something—to be somebody.
   Empty shells who were once useful, creative, and lovable,
      but who now chose not to exist
         because it is easier.
   Empty shells who were created to love,

but who had chosen not to
        because it takes commitment to love.
Empty shells who once had an adventuresome spirit,
        but who now chose to be neutral
            because it is safer.

I found a place called neutrality,
    A place that is in-between.

I stood and looked
    to the land of neutrality...
    then to the land of commitment...
    and again and again to each.
Did I really want what I had found?

Decisions—

    Decisions—

        Decisions—

                                —Ted R. Witt

"You can only protect your liberties in this world by protecting the other [person's] freedom. You can only be free if I am free. The same thing that would get me may be used to get you...."

                                —Clarence Darrow

THE RICH YOUNG RULER[15]

"What must I do, master, to gain
        Eternal life?
From my youth I have kept the Commandments,
Honoured my parents;
Theft, murder, lying, adultery—
All these
By God's mercy have passed me by.
What then must I do, master?
What more must I do?"

"Sell all," he replied, "and follow me."
An easy saying.
He, a carpenter, a carpenter's son,
Sacrificed nothing.
And his man Peter—smirking, self-righteous—
What did he lose
But some worn nets, a boat-share,
And trade in the market?
It wasn't myself I was thinking of—
Ease and possessions—

83

But the responsibility of wealth
Towards its dependents.
What of them, if I had obeyed him—
What of my servants?

That's what I tell myself, now—
But do I believe it?
Then—silent—I walked away,
Watching my sandals,
While his voice, the voice of my heart,
Followed me homeward.
In misery, I stopped by the lake.
Hid by the crowd-wall,
I heard him speak of the Kingdom of God,
the camel, the needle.

A SPRINGBOARD FOR INDEPENDENCE

If we accept the fact that children must go through the transition to an independent life, we realize that they need roots which can take hold in any soil. The roots of personal life are the relationships which persons have with one another. For example, children may never be allowed to make their own decisions. They may grow up in an atmosphere where parents either decide for them or subtly manipulate them into doing what they want. The children never learn to take responsibility for decisions and actions. They do not learn to allocate their money or buy their clothes. They think that they are making up their own minds only to see in retrospect that parents jockeyed them into their way of thinking. The lives of the children have been rooted deeply in dependence upon parents. They know what is right. Children know nothing. As these children mature and move into other groups, they will either look back to parents for guidance or find some other adult on whom they can lean. They will not take responsibility for their own lives. They will never achieve independence. They have not been given roots which can take hold in any new soil, because they are merely carrying their relations to their parents into every new situation and transforming associates into substitute parents.[16]

Notes

1. From *Times Three* by Phyllis McGinley. Copyright © 1960 by Phyllis McGinley. Reprinted by permission of Viking Penguin Inc.

2. Reuel Howe, *Herein Is Love* (Valley Forge, Pa.: Judson Press, 1961), p. 27.

3. Adapted from *Camping in Covenant Community* by Geneva Giese (Richmond, Va.: CLC Press, 1965), pp. 113–114.

4. Adapted from an address by Joseph Sittler, published in the *Proceedings of the National Symposium on the Church Outdoors* sponsored by the Church Camp Council of the American Camping Association, October 1973.

5. Steve Van Matre, *Acclimatizing* (Martinsville, Ind.: American Camping Association, 1974), p. 47.

6. Reuel Howe, *Man's Need and God's Action* (New York: The Seabury Press, 1953), p. 145.

7. Adapted from *Into Parenthood,* by Donald G. and Bernice M. Wright (pp. 53–54). Copyright © by Graded Press. Used by permission.

8. James Aggrey in the *Young America Basic Reading Program,* Level 15, by Leo Fay and Myron L. Coulter (New York: Phelps-Stokes Fund; Chicago: Rand McNally & Co.), pp. 512–513.

9. Paul Tillich, *The Shaking of the Foundations* (New York: Charles Scribner's Sons, 1948), pp. 161–162.

10. Tillich, *Shaking of the Foundations,* p. 162.

11. Harvey Broome, *Out Under the Sky of the Great Smokies* (Knoxville, Tenn.: Greenbrier Press, 1975), pp. 20–21.

12. John H. Westerhoff, III, *How Can We Teach Values* (Philadelphia: United Church Press, 1969).

13. Adapted from *Values Clarification* by Sidney Simon, Leland W. Howe and Howard Kirschenbaum (New York: Hart Publishing Co., 1972), pp. 94–97.

14. Adapted from *Meeting Yourself Halfway* by Sidney B. Simon (Niles, Ill.: Argus Communications, 1974), pp. 66–70.

15. Clive Sansom, *The Witnesses and Other Poems* (London: Methuen & Co., 1956), pp. 29–30. Used by permission.

16. Excerpted from *Love and Conflict,* by Gibson Winter. Copyright © 1958 by Gibson Winter. Reprinted by permission of Doubleday & Company, Inc.

Part III
Resources

1. GET-ACQUAINTED ACTIVITIES

The first few hours of camp are, in many ways, the most important of the total experience. The campers will be apprehensive about the experience and will be covertly asking many questions about what it is they have gotten themselves into. Their anxiety will usually revolve around two kinds of concerns: (1) mechanical concerns, such as the site and procedures, and (2) relational concerns about getting along with the other members of the group.

The first concerns can be cared for in a brief period of orientation with the campers. In such a session the following items will need to be given consideration. In addition, do not forget to mention those concerns that are unique to your campsite or program.

The living quarters: selection of bunk; making bed; storing personal belongings; keeping clean; and, if canvas quarters, care of ropes and canvas.

The environment: care of area; what to cut and not to cut; conservation of plants, flowers, insects, etc.; presence of night sounds, animals, etc.

Food service: plan for setting and clearing tables if meals are in dining area; if small group cooking, plans for menu planning, preparation, etc.

Personal health care: arrangements for brushing teeth, showers, etc.; health center or nurse; first aid kits and use of them.

Safety: hazards in camp and ways to avoid them (plants, animals, insects, etc.); fire prevention, precautions and what to do in case of fire; use of camp tools and equipment (axes, saws, etc.).

Personal conduct: what is expected of campers; what camper can expect of counselor; quiet time and bedtime behavior; individual's role in group; camp rules.

Knowing the camp policies is important if the campers are to feel at ease in the new setting. It is even more important for the junior highs to feel comfortable with the people around them. The following activities will be helpful in getting the group to become acquainted.

MILLING

Give each camper a sheet of paper and a crayon or felt-tip pen. Ask the campers to write their names and three of the following things on the paper.

—Three words that describe you
—Your favorite hobby

—A picture of yourself
—Your favorite bird, tree, or other nature object
—Your favorite camp activity
—Your favorite school subject
—Your pets

Campers pin the papers on themselves where they can be easily seen, then walk around and read the other papers. Encourage campers to talk about the things they read.

MILLING QUIZ
After milling, the leader collects everyone's paper, reads characteristics of individuals, and sees who can give the person's name from the clues given.

DYADS
Have campers, after milling, choose someone with whom they would like to get better acquainted. Have campers tell why they chose each other and share more about themselves. Be sure nobody is left out.

After dyads have had a chance to get better acquainted, have two dyads get together. Follow the doubling procedure until the total group is together.

CONCENTRIC CIRCLES
After milling, form two circles, one inside the other. Have the outer circle face in and the inner circle face out. Partners will be formed. Give two minutes for partners to discuss their milling papers. Rotate to new partners until everyone in the outer circle has had opportunity to be partner to those in the inner circle.

OPENING DISCUSSIONS
Start discussions centered around some of the following questions:

—Why did you come to camp?
—What do you like best about camp?
—What would you like to accomplish at camp?
—What bothers you most about being at camp?
—What can you offer to the camp experience?

OPEN-ENDED SENTENCES
Have campers select a partner. With campers in pairs, give them an open-ended sentence and ask them to complete the sentence with the first thought that comes to mind. When they have finished, have them change

partners and give them another open-ended sentence. Do this until everyone has been with everyone else. Some suggested sentences are:

> My hobbies are _____.
> My favorite song, movie, food, etc., is _____.
> When at camp, I _____.
> A good camp counselor is _____.
> I feel good when _____.
> My friends _____.
> It feels good when I _____.
> I cry if _____.
> My parents _____.
> I get mad when _____.
> Groups make me feel _____.
> Junior high young people are _____.
> The most important thing in life is _____.
> The thing about which I worry most is _____.
> The church should _____.
> I think I am too _____.
> I feel embarrassed when _____.
> I trust people who _____.
> The hardest thing I have to do is _____.
> Church means most to me when _____.

Give campers a chance to discuss their replies in the total group.

2. WORSHIP

1) Teachable moments provide many opportunities for spontaneous worship. Be alert for times of worship in response to the group's unfolding awareness of God—when discovering something of particular beauty in nature, when feeling gratitude for the coolness of a refreshing rain, when awestruck at the magnitude of creation during a stargaze, or when experiencing the joy of friendship felt at the completion of a jointly-done project. These special moments can be some of the most meaningful experienced in camp. At times the counselor may be wise to actually "name the name" of worship in order to help junior highs realize that worship can occur in settings different from those generally considered to be worshipful. Such spontaneous worship may be as simple as this.

Joey: I'm tired and hot after the hike. It's good to sit under this shade tree to rest and cool off.

Leader: Trees are good for resting under, aren't they? They certainly provide a lot of other things for us too. I'm glad that God made trees! Let's all say together, "Thank you, God, for shade trees."

All: *(in unison)* Thank you, God, for shade trees.

Leader: Giving thanks to God is part of our worship, and perhaps we should be more aware of the many gifts that God has given.

2) Planned periods for worship should also be part of the camp experience. These times may be planned for individuals, for small groups, and on some occasions for the total camp. In all cases the worship should be an expression of some facet of the experiences of the camper during camp, a direct outgrowth of a camp experience rather than something planned far ahead of camp. Whenever possible, campers should be involved in planning and leading these worship times. One of the objectives of camp worship should be to help campers realize that worship is something we do—not something we sit and simply watch.

As an example of the way a planned worship may evolve out of a group's experience, let us continue the dialogue described just above.

Leader: What are some of those gifts? Can you name some?

Group members: *(several suggestions)*

Leader: I tell you what let's do, let's take these things you've named and create a litany to have as a prayer at mealtime.

Sue: What's a litany?

Leader: Let me show you. . . .

Thus, the sensitive leader has taken one comment, had an unplanned time of worship, created opportunity to teach a group about a litany, and has the door open for the group to create an expression of their gratitude to share with the total camp in a planned time of worship.

a) Opportunities for individual worship may be included on a regular basis in the daily schedule. These might be morning watch, or other periods during the day set aside for individual "alone" time. Some guidance should be given—either written or verbal. Junior highs will respond more favorably if they have a specific task to accomplish, an idea to think about, or a selection to read.

b) Small group or shelter group worship is most often done during a rest time, around a nightly campfire, or after all are in bed. These opportunities may be more spontaneous, growing out of the experiences of the day. In some camps, all worship will be delegated to the small group. In that case, the leaders will need to help the group be aware of the opportunities for worship. The small groups may want to do such things as sing hymns, compose prayers, poems, litanies. Settings may include a sunrise or sunset vesper service, a special service to celebrate a significant event in the life of the group, an echo sing across a lake or from hill to hill, a campfire, a closing night dedication or communion, and many others determined by the site and the experiences of the group.

c) Total camp worship is usually planned by the director of the camp and sometimes is aided by small groups. Many of the settings may be the same as for the small group. In addition, some of the more traditional services such as Holy Communion or a footwashing may be celebrated.

3) Resources for worship are varied. In planning, leaders think immediately of Scripture, prayer, and music. There are many other possibilities, such as: use of drama *(write your own or read play excerpts, role-play, act out Bible stories or parables);* movement *(act out, without words, the Lord's prayer or other Bible passages);* storytelling *(Bible, traditional hero stories, or open-ended tales which campers can complete);* litanies *(excellent ones in traditional services of worship, or have the group create their own);* creeds *(traditional ones or one created by the small group);* poetry; art.

Even in the use of the more traditional forms, much creativity can be used to make the worship more vital to the campers. Scriptures may be adapted to choral readings, made more relevant by paraphrasing, acted out, chanted, or used as the basis for developing prayers, litanies, or responsive readings. Prayers may be written for use in a variety of settings, such as morning praise, meal blessings, and times of thanksgiving, confession, dedication, and intercession. Leaders can do a great deal to encourage youth to express their faith through prayer. The use of music has traditionally been a major part of camp program. Hymns should be taught to a group before the worship experience. Careful thought should be given to content and movement. Hymns may be sung or read in unison. Hymn interpretations can be helpful. Some small groups may write their own hymn or teach a new hymn to the rest of the camp.

3. EXPLORATIONS AND DISCOVERIES

In making maximum use of the outdoor setting of the camp, the role of exploration, discovery, and adventure activities will be significant. The junior high camper has an adventuresome spirit, and a wise leader is one who takes advantage of this characteristic. Below you will find two kinds of material. The first is simply a list of possible activities that might be done in your small group. The second is a detailed description of several activities. It is expected that each activity chosen by the small group would help accomplish the objectives of the camp and that detailed planning and specific objective setting for the experience would be a small group task.

Take orientation and exploration hikes around the camp property.

Select a site for development of a small group area for cooking, campfires, sleeping out, and using campcraft skills.

Develop the outdoor site with fireplace, shelter, tables, or other needs.

Take discovery hikes on specific topics: plants, trees, land formation, birds, etc.

Cookout: planning menus, food orders, preparation, and cleanup.

Overnight campout: planning, erecting shelters, meals, sanitation, fire craft.

Tree identification using keys and games.

Follow animal tracks; make track casts.

Study stumps.

Fish for a meal together.

Take a hike to study erosion and select a project to help prevent or correct erosion.

Take a night hike to study sounds, animals, or stars.

Make weather observations and keep a log of weather conditions.

Forecast weather for camp.

Creek hike.

Select and carry through on a "camp improvement project."

Learn to identify bird songs.

"Animal home" hike.

Watch a sunrise or sunset.

Explore a lake, stream, pond, or puddle.

Geology hike: fossils, quarry, or cut in nearby road.

Construct a nature trail in the camp.

Construct a sundial.

Build and use an Indian loom.

Conduct some Acclimatizing Activities (see bibliography).

Make an ant house.

SHARPEN THE SENSES[1]

1. How many homes can you find? *(rabbit log, bird's nest)*
2. How many tracks, signs, or traces of animals can you find? *(horse tracks, rabbit scat)*
3. How many signs of homemaking can you find? *(spider weaving a web)*
4. How many plants can you find one inch high or less? *(Don't dig them up!)*
5. How many signs of human presence can you find? *(rubbish, fences)*
6. What can you find under dead wood? Dead bark? Rocks?
7. What can you find in the stream or lake? *(Use a net, strainer, or handkerchief.)*
8. How many forms of life would not be here if it were not for the constant water supply?
9. Find the following: a tree that has thorns, one that is dead, one that is dying, one that has dancing leaves.
10. What signs can you find that once there was nothing green living in this area? *(fossils of sea animals)*
11. How many different "feels" can you find? *(smooth leaves, rough bark)*
12. How many odors can you smell? *(dank soil, green grass)*
13. How many colors can you find? *(blue sky, pink flowers)*
14. How many sounds can you hear? *(birds singing, leaves rustling)*
15. Can you find any pitfalls for the unwary? *(spider web, doodlebug)*
16. Can you find any signs of accidents or untimely ends? *(tree burned)*
17. How many discards can you find? *(insect shells, snake skins)*
18. What do you see moving? *(birds, clouds)*
19. What means for planting seeds can you see or do you already know? *(squirrel—acorns; birds—grass and flower seeds)*
20. How many parasites can you find? *(living at the expense of another—mistletoe, fungi)*

A COMPASS HIKE

The compass depends on natural laws, and a compass hike often contributes to campers' understanding of the dependability of the natural world. A group of twelve should have at least four compasses, and it is better if only two hikers share a compass. The type compass that is best is one with a plastic base having a directional arrow and a needle housing that can be turned to bring different degrees in line with the directional arrow.

Introduce certain fundamentals at the beginning of a hike. Let each camper practice using a compass. Let the campers first set a compass due north. Then demonstrate how to set the compass to travel east, south, west, and intermediate directions.

Next show the campers how to walk a square. Set the compass on north and walk a given number of steps northward. Next, set the compass to east and take the same number of steps in that direction. Set the compass south and west, walking the same number of steps in those directions. *(Each group might be directed to walk a different number of steps; this will demonstrate the fact that all would return to the same point of beginning.)* Next you might demonstrate how to walk an equilateral triangle.

Show the campers how to *pace. (A pace is two steps.)* Measure a one-hundred- or two-hundred-foot line on as level land as is conveniently near. Have each camper walk this distance four times, counting two steps as one. *(Be sure that these are regular walking steps and not stretched-out steps.)* Take the average for the four walks and divide this number into the distance paced. The result is the number of feet and inches in an individual's pace. With each hiker in possession of information about the length of his or her own pace, you will be able to give directions in feet to be traveled without having to sight a visible object each time.

Campers enjoy setting the course of a compass hike for others to follow. You may do this by exchanging compass hikes with another small group, or you may divide your own small group into two groups. Let one group sight the landmarks and write directions, such as, "Go for 65 feet at an angle of 238 degrees to a fallen oak tree. Go at an angle of 167 degrees to a clump of five pines. Then go at an angle of 24 degrees to a white oak with a squirrel's nest. Finally, go at an angle of 180 degrees to a large boulder." The course-setting group can then give the compass hike directions and compasses to the other group to follow. It is fun to combine a compass hike with a treasure hunt or to direct a group to some interesting item. One campsite had directions by compass for a destination hike to a sawmill at which the owners welcomed the campers.

If a topographical map of your campsite is available, teach the campers how to orient it to true north by using the declension scale at the bottom of the map. Then choose a high hill, a deep ravine, a particular place on a stream, or some landmark in the area covered by the map, and run a direct course to it. You might even estimate the distance and pace it off, if it is not too far from your living area.

To learn how to use a compass, you may need the help of a resource person in the pre-camp training session. Keep in mind the abilities of members of your group as you teach them to use a compass.

STARGAZING

The stars will seem brighter to you and your campers when you are away from the interference of city lights. It is likely that your campers will suggest a stargaze, which can be done with or without a telescope. Because only one person can look through a telescope at a time, it is wise to have star charts ready to allow the other campers to locate the constellations. Stargazing takes preparation. The campers could work in groups of two to make constellation charts of those constellations they hope to identify. Take a piece of dark construction paper, and with pencil point make small holes in the shape of the constellation. At the stargaze shine a flashlight through the holes. Then point to the location of the constellation in the sky. If you know what you are looking for, you are more likely to find it! To add interest, each group might give the story of their constellation or of a star in the constellation.

You may want to close your stargaze with a service of worship that points beyond creation to its Creator. Psalm 8 is often used because it points to the value of humanity in God's creation as compared to the stars. The Pleiades and Orion are referred to in Amos 5:8. Unfortunately, Orion cannot be seen in the summer sky. Pleiades, sometimes known as the seven sisters, is also a winter constellation; but it is low on the horizon from about the middle of August. It is very helpful to have a star wheel which can be set to the date and hour of observation. This helps you know what constellations you have a possibility of seeing. It can be very frustrating to look for a constellation that is not even above the horizon at a particular time of night or during a particular season.

4. CAMPCRAFT

One of the most valuable activities for a junior high camp small group will be the development of a group living area away from the main camp area. It gives the group the opportunity to learn valuable outdoor living skills.

As campers develop their living area, they gain a sense of contributing to the well-being of future campers as well as to the comfort of their own group. Deciding which things should be built first teaches the need for setting priorities and for setting up work schedules. Often the need to substitute materials for those recommended encourages creative thinking. The satisfaction that comes from the construction of something useful is probably the chief value realized in working on a living area.

It is here in the small group living area that the campers will spend much of their time—working, planning, playing, studying, discussing, worshiping, cooking, sleeping out.

Selecting A Site

In some camps, each group is allowed to choose its own site and develop it according to its own desires, with due regard for preserving the natural beauty of the area, privacy from other groups, distance from the main camp area, availability of water and firewood, and other necessary considerations. To choose such a site means exploration of available camp areas, discussions and evaluations, and finally a group decision.

In other camps, sites have been selected and partially developed, and each small group is assigned the use of one. A new group may be helped to feel a sense of stewardship toward its campsite which deepens the group members' identification with it. Realizing that the campers before them have developed it thus far and left it in good condition for them to use increases the new group's desire to improve it for its own enjoyment and to leave the site even better for those who will follow.

Equipment Needed

For construction of the small group living area a small group should have at least the following equipment, tools, and supplies available:

Hand saw	Shovel
Buck saw	Rake
Ax	Mattock-pick
Wedge for splitting logs	Sharpening stone
Pocket knives	Binder twine
First aid kit	Tarps

What to Construct

Construct what is needed in relationship to what the small group will be doing in the area. If cookouts are planned, it will call for an area to prepare, cook, and serve meals. If sleepouts are planned, then shelter is required. Below are listed several possible projects in developing a living area.

1. Select and clear fire circle.
2. Build a fireplace.
3. Build tables for food preparation.
4. Select and make woodcutting area: sawbuck for sawing logs, chopping block, wood storage rack.
5. Arrange stones or logs for sitting.

6. Build racks and shelves for storage of food.
7. Make tool storage area.
8. Make canvas shelter.
9. Make latrines, handwashing arrangement.
10. Make fire circle for fellowship.
11. Make worship area.

Protecting the Area

Here are a few stewardship facts to remember in camp construction:

1. Cut only saplings that are needed and will be used.
2. Choose saplings that are crowded by others, stunted in growth, or for other reasons have little chance of making timber trees.
3. Make a clean cut with a saw as near the ground as possible—do not leave pointed stob to injure other people.
4. Select saplings from a wide area so as not to deplete any one area unduly.
5. Avoid overclearing undergrowth which is useful in holding soil and in giving a screen of privacy.
6. Run paths on contour of hills instead of straight up the grade, so as to prevent erosion.
7. Keep paths to a minimum—avoid having paths all over the woods.
8. Mark trails, if necessary, with stones, or with paper tied to trees. Never blaze a tree—this is not done today, as a blaze is a wound that

RESPONSIBLE WITH CREATION

hurts a tree as much as a cut on a person's leg hurts.

9. Avoid contaminating small streams by dumping garbage and refuse into them. Dig a pit, or burn garbage.

Specific Projects

TARP FOR PROTECTION

Before erecting a tarp, lead the campers in considering such things as prevailing winds and rain directions, drainage, and sun. Usually a tarp is stretched over three ridgepoles lashed horizontally to trees or held in place by upright poles. The tarp should be so placed that the low side will drain off and away from the living area. Sometimes another tarp is dropped down one side as protection against blowing rain. Do not drive nails or tacks into canvas. Rather, tie it with cord or binder's twine to keep it in place. Avoid touching canvas when it is wet. Handling it breaks the air bubbles that make canvas waterproof, and may result in a leak. A tarp should be located so that branches of trees will not rub against the canvas.

DINING TABLE AND BENCHES

A dining table may be made by lashing small saplings to a support frame of logs. The saplings must be relatively straight and about the same diameter to make the table level and usable. Lashing instructions are found in Catherine Hammett's *Your Own Book of Campcraft (see bibliography)*. If you must conserve saplings at your campsite, or if frequent

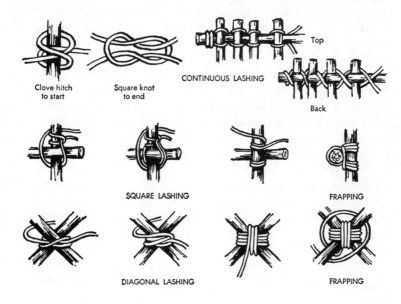

Clove hitch to start   Square knot to end   CONTINUOUS LASHING   Top

Back

SQUARE LASHING   FRAPPING

DIAGONAL LASHING   FRAPPING

eating out-of-doors necessitates a more level table, it is often advisable to construct tables and benches of one-by-eight-inch boards and two-by-fours. At one semi-desert campsite young people made forms and poured two-by-four-foot concrete slabs about two inches thick. They placed three of these across supports made of two-by-fours. The durable table so made was easily washed down and kept sanitary. *(They also used the concrete slabs for constructing a food preparation center and a dishwashing area.)* Be sure that your table is of the correct height, no matter what construction you use. The needs of most campers are well served by a table height of thirty inches and a bench height of seventeen inches.

Illustrated on page 99 are ways to lash. Learn to do these.

SEATS OF LOGS, BOARD, OR STONE

To raise a log off the ground for more comfortable seating use X-shaped braces made by lashing two logs together. Or, let a short length of a log rest on its side and cut a groove into it to hold the seating log steady. Strip logs of their bark; this will lessen destruction by insects. Logs do not need to be from living trees. Many times portions of a recently fallen or dead tree will supply logs that are not burned or diseased. In some sections of the country, it is better stewardship to buy grade three lumber boards and two-by-fours for use in constructing benches than it is to cut timber. Consult with your camp manager before cutting trees. The forestry or agricultural agent in your section is a specialist who will be glad to talk with you and your campers about which trees may be cut and which should not be cut. Stools and individual seats can be made from split logs or a crosscut section of a tree into which legs are wedged.

TOOL RACK

Tools should never be left lying on the ground and should always be put back into place when not in use. This is not only for safety's sake but for quick location in times of emergency. A shovel is a fire-fighting weapon as well as a digging tool. A fire could get out of hand while you looked for a carelessly thrown aside shovel. A tool rack is a valuable facility in a camp. To make one, space two limbs about three inches apart and lash them to a tree. *(At intervals of about six inches, limbs may be lashed crosswise.)* Tools can then be inserted between the limbs so spaced and thus be suspended from the ground. *(Always replace the sheath of an ax before returning it to the rack.)* The tool rack should have a cover to protect the tools from rain.

FOOD PREPARATION CENTER

Having a separate table for food preparation is a good practice in

 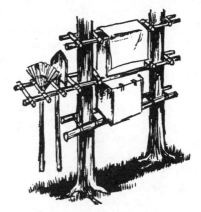

sanitation. Such a center can be made by lashing limbs to form a table area between trees, by forming a tripod and lashing saplings to form a table, or by using lumber. Again recognize the best working height—from thirty-two to thirty-six inches.

DISHWASHING CENTER

A dishwashing center should be constructed so as to facilitate a seven-phase process: (1) scraping and disposing of garbage and grease, (2) systematic stacking, (3) washing, (4) rinsing, (5) sanitizing, (6) drying

(using mesh bags for dishes, a drip can for silver, and a towel for utensils), and (7) disposal of dishwater. The dishwashing table should be about thirty-two inches high so that unnecessary lifting and bending will not be required. At one end of the assembly have two garbage cans for wet and dry garbage. Have an area for stacking dishes. Then allow space for a wash pan, a rinse pan, and a working surface on which may be placed mesh bags as they are filled with dishes. Nearby should be a hot fire on which is placed the sanitizing can. This should be large enough for submerging the mesh bags. Add the proper amount of chlorine to the water and boil the dishes in it for three minutes. Nearby should be a dishdrying tripod or pole onto which the sacks can be hung to air. Turn cups carefully to drain water out. Wipe utensils with paper towels or cloth towels and turn them upside down on a lashed table, to permit air to circulate. Following this procedure will greatly reduce the drudgery of dishwashing. Building a separate fire for dishwashing is advisable because cooking is never done over a hot fire. If you wait to build the fire up after the cooking is through, the dishwashers are delayed, because a large amount of water takes time to come to a boil.

SHELTER CONSTRUCTION

No other camp experience brings a deeper sense of being at home in the natural world and draws a group closer together in fellowship than sleeping outdoors in rustic shelters, and junior highs thrill to the experience. Even timid campers find the experience meaningful in the security of their group. Some camps may wish to build the more permanent rustic shelters like hogans, made from saplings bent covered-wagon fashion over either the ground or a plank flooring, and covered with a large canvas tarpaulin. Use a 1″ pipe to make holes in the ground and place the 1″ green saplings with ends trimmed to 1″ in these holes. On a wooden floor drill 1″ holes and run the saplings through the holes for stationary support.

Small groups who do not have any sleeping facilities at their campsites may wish to construct simple shelters for their times of sleeping outdoors, such as the ones illustrated. The simplest shelter of all is made by stretching a rope between trees or other uprights and hanging a tarpaulin over it, staking its bottom edges to the ground in pup-tent fashion. Tab tents of the 10′ × 12′ size are an ideal size to use since they are easily handled by campers, need no poles as they are suspended from trees or other existing supports, and are of adequate size. Allow about 40 square feet per camper for living under canvas. Simple shelters to build are the hogan or covered wagon, the lean-to, the round-to, and the A-frame. Wood for shelters may be saplings (1″ to 2″ in diameter and cut with regard to good conservation practices), bamboo poles, or 2″ × 2″ lumber like clothesline poles. Either tab tents or regular tarps can be used with these.

102

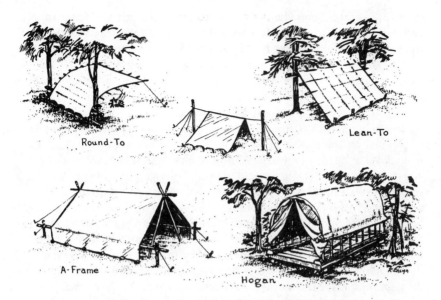

Round-To

Lean-To

A-Frame

Hogan

Shelter supports are lashed with strong binder twine. For lashing instructions refer to Catherine T. Hammett's *Your Own Book of Campcraft,* Chapter 8. Shelters will usually need to be ditched to prevent water from soaking the ground within them.

SLEEP-OUTS

A sleep-out should not be attempted too soon. Be sure your group is ready and prepares well. Comfort is a requisite for a good night's sleep, and this is as true of sleeping outdoors as elsewhere. A little extra time spent making a place comfortable for sleeping is worth the effort. This means choosing a place that is free of humps, be they rock or pebbles, roots, or clumps of grass. Leaves, pine needles, cut grass, and moss placed under the ground cloth make the ground more comfortable. Many campers, particularly those who sleep on their sides, like to dig a slight depression in the ground where their hips come. If the sleep-out takes place in camp at the small group campsite or near the cabins, take your pillow along!

A ground cover to keep out dampness may be a poncho, waterproof canvas, an old plastic tablecloth, or a length of plastic that is available. Some camps provide the last. A bedroll is easily made with two or three blankets, folded together and pinned. When sleeping outdoors, it is necessary to have as much cover underneath as on top. A mosquito net is a necessity in many camps and can be stretched over lashed supports set in the ground over the bedroll.

Latrines should be dug conveniently close to the sleeping areas, being careful to locate them where they will not contaminate the water supply and where there is privacy. If bushes do not screen the area adequately a simple screen of old canvas, burlap bags, or brush can be lashed around it. Pile the dirt behind the trench that is dug and keep a shovel handy. Everytime the latrine is used the waste should be covered with some dirt.

WOODCUTTING AREA

Every living area needs a woodcutting area. Locate the area in a place convenient to the cooking and campfire areas. The area should be relatively level and free of loose rocks and debris. It should be clear of shrubs and overhanging limbs that would obstruct the swing of an ax. To test this, let the tallest camper try out the arc of the ax swing overhead and parallel to the ground. Allow two extra feet for safety. The area, of course, should not be in a normal path of travel. Set the area aside by a simply-lashed fence or by a binder twine rope, so that a person could not wander into it unaware. Instruct woodcutters always to swing away from the activity area.

To make a sawbuck take two stakes about three or four inches in diameter and drive them into the ground to form an X. Do the same thing with two other stakes placed two feet away. To make them firm, lash each pair of stakes where they cross. To brace the two X's, lash sticks on both sides of each of them. *(These will also serve to hold logs of less than three feet in length as they are cut.)*

A wood storage rack is a useful facility. Build the rack up off the ground so that it will be dry and so that the danger of snakes hiding in the pile will be less. You will need three types of wood: (1) tinder—twigs the thickness of matchsticks, or shavings, or thin bark; (2) kindling—pieces six to twelve inches long and as big around as your thumb; and (3) fuel—split logs and good-sized branches from hardwood trees. These should be separated and neatly stacked. Use a canvas or plastic cover to protect the stack from rain. Locate your wood stack close enough to the fire for convenience but not so close that sparks could ignite it.

TALK-IT-OVER AREA

Using logs, make a circle large enough to accommodate the group without crowding. To avoid sitting too close to the fire, it may be better to place the logs in an intimate semicircle with the fire some distance away in the open end. Heat from the fire can be reduced by placing it in a trench. When you build a talk-it-over fire make it no larger than necessary. Use only those logs that are small enough to burn completely in the time you will be around the fire. For fire prevention, wet smoldering logs down thoroughly and cover them completely with dirt when you leave your talk-it-over circle. As you plan, think about the time of day or evening when your circle

RESPONSIBLE WITH CREATION

will be used and the climate of your section of the country. In warm climates it is foolish to locate a circle in a low spot surrounded by dense growth that will cut off all breezes. In cool climates you may need protection from night breezes.

USE AND CARE OF TOOLS

The pocketknife and ax are indispensable tools in camp, but they are also potentially dangerous. Know how to use them and care for them.

The Pocketknife

1. Buy a good steel knife. Keep it clean, dry, and free of rust.
2. Keep it sharp. You are more apt to get cut trying to make a dull knife work than by a sharp knife that cuts as you want it to. Learn how to sharpen your knife.
3. Whittle away from you with due regard for the sweep of the blade when it leaves the wood you are cutting.
4. Don't walk with an open knife.
5. When finished with it (even momentarily) close it and put it in your pocket. You won't lose it, and you won't risk cutting yourself by absent-mindedly leaning or sitting on an open knife.
6. Pass an open knife only when necessary, and then with the cutting edge of the blade away from the hand and the handle toward the receiver.

The Ax

1. Keep it sharp. Use a chopping block of solid wood to cut your wood on whenever possible. It will save nicking the cutting edge of your ax. Never chop a piece of wood on the ground where rocks may nick it. Sharpening an ax blade is a tedious filing job.
2. Sheathe an ax when it is not in use. Keep it dry. During a clear day when the ax will be used a lot it can be kept in a chopping block. Never leave it in a block overnight as the block will swell with the night moisture and make it difficult to remove the ax.
3. When chopping be sure no branches, ropes, or other obstructions are in the way to catch and throw your ax. Aim your blow and keep your eyes on where you want to hit. Chop diagonally into wood, never straight in. Cut away from the butt of the tree or branch. Always place wood to be cut on opposite side of chop block from your toes, and bend in knees enough so hands come below your knees at end of swing, thus ensuring that your foot or leg will not be chopped.

More specific help for using and caring for these tools is found in Chapter 9 of Catherine T. Hammett's *Your Own Book of Campcraft*. All tools used by the small group, including craft equipment, should be used with a sense of stewardship; this means using them properly, and putting them away carefully when finished, so that they will be in good condition for the next campers who will use them.

5. NATURE CRAFTS

Camp provides optimum opportunity to utilize nature materials as a resource in meeting the objectives of the camp. The crafts program should make maximum use of rocks, wood, leaves, twigs, nuts, seeds, weeds, animal tracks, and innumerable other objects which are found locally and are usable in creating craft objects. It is best if the crafts program is a small group activity, planned by the group and evolving from the life of the group itself. *(Recall our discussion on the holistic approach?)*

The use of native craft objects has several advantages over the "manufactured" crafts:

—Less expensive, since there is a minimum of imported supplies such as glue, paper, paste, crayons, felt-tip markers, inks, paints, and simple tools.

—Requires less space, since they may usually be done in the small group area.

—Small group leaders have skills to assist with crafts.

—Collection of materials becomes a program element which will require observation and movement around the area where the collection is permitted.

—The results of the craft activity will be more than merely something to take home to show "what I made at camp." The results are expected to include an increased knowledge, appreciation and understanding of the surroundings, the environmental quality, ecological significance and God's plan for nature's operation.

—Gives a camper the opportunity to create a work of beauty and to have a positive part in creating something decorative or useful.

Several books are listed in the bibliography which give numerous possible craft ideas. The ones which follow are merely a sampling, using a variety of materials and techniques.

PAINT WITH FLOWERS AND GRASSES

If flowers are abundant in your camp area, you may be able to pick some flowers without harm to the world around you. Rub the crushed petals over paper to paint a picture. Often the color given by the crushed petal is not the same as that of the blossom. Grasses and leaves will yield many different shades of greens and browns. Limit the size of your work to dimensions of about six by eight inches.

ANIMAL TRACK CASTS

Often bird watchers find other things along the path which may be obliterated by trail traffic. Animal tracks may be preserved in plaster. If you want your plaque to have a shape, make a round or square frame by pushing cardboard strips vertically into the earth around the track. With tweezers carefully remove trash that may have fallen into the track. Pour plaster around the edge and let it spread into the tracks. After the plaster hardens, remove the cardboard frame.

SPIDER WEB PRINTS

The intricate design of a spider web can be made into a picture. Make sure the spider is not in its web. Carefully spray the web on both sides with light-colored enamel paint. Then bring a piece of dark paper under the web or back of the web so that the sprayed web adheres to the paper. Clip the strands of the web which secure it, being careful not to pull the web pattern out of shape. A beautiful Chinese print worth framing can be made by spraying the web with gold paint and collecting it on white rice paper. Make several web prints before you try this.

CLAY MODELING

If there is native clay on your campsite, gather some in a bucket and cover it with a wet cloth to keep it in a pliable condition. Give campers a tin can or piece of board on which to rest their work, and let them form the clay into realistic or surrealistic shapes. Let the way something looks or the way the campers feel be their guide in what they do. A damp cloth placed over an incomplete work will permit the camper to resume at a later time. Clay modeling is a wonderful rainy day activity.

ROCK SCULPTURE

Interesting sculpture can be made by gluing small stones together into shapes. Even those who think themselves without talent find this fun. Use a glue that dries clear. Stones may be chipped into pieces or used whole. If shells are native to your campsite, these can also be made into sculptures.

SAND AND SOIL PAINTING

Collect different colors of soil from around your campsite. Draw a design on paper or cardboard. Cover a small portion with a glue that will dry clear. Carefully sprinkle your design with the desired color of soil.

Allow the painting to set a few minutes and then gently pour off excess soil. Repeat this process for each portion and color.

NATURAL COLLAGE

Similar to sand or soil painting is the natural collage, which may be made with all sorts of barks, crushed leaves, stones, shells, burls, vines, and dried flowers, in combination. *("Collage" is a French term which means pasted paper.)* Burlap stretched over cardboard makes an appropriate background, or the collage may be made on a piece of plywood. After completing your design, spray it with clear shellac or plastic. A collage may represent reality or express feelings. Many collages are works of art worthy of framing and hanging.

A TERRARIUM

Small plants, mosses, and barks or rocks with lichen can be arranged in a glass gallon jar. Turn the jar on its side. In the bottom, place an inch layer of crushed charcoal. Add an inch layer of topsoil. Arrange the plants. Water carefully, and screw on the lid. A small stick placed on either side of the jar will prevent it from rolling.

6. OUTDOOR COOKING

OUTDOOR COOKERY[2]

Half the fun of campin' out
   And trampin' here and there
Is building up your appetite
   'Til you're hungry as a bear.

Then sitt'n down at mess time
   With swell victuals all about—
Boy! That's livin' what is livin'
   And you get it campin' out!

Cooking in the outdoors is one of the most exciting parts of camp life. It can be a learning experience while also serving as an element of fun and providing for basic needs. Many junior highs have had little or no experience with planning and preparing meals. Cooking meals within the small group can help the group feel a sense of accomplishment and build group spirit. In planning and preparing a meal each camper needs to have a specific responsibility. In this way campers can learn to feel what it means to have someone depending on them.

When planning for a cookout keep in mind the following things:

1) Plan a balanced menu.

     RESPONSIBLE WITH CREATION

2) Plan a menu that does not require cooking techniques or skills beyond the level of the campers. On the other hand, plan for styles of cooking that challenge the campers to try new things.

3) Remember the budget limitations of the camp. Many camps provide counselors with a list of available food supplies with costs and require that small groups live within a specified budget.

4) Consider the kind of cooking equipment and utensils needed.

5) Consider the type of fire(s) needed and kinds of wood needed.

6) Remember that preparing a meal takes a certain amount of time and that the menu items should be able to be prepared in the time available. Don't forget that a part of cooking out is also gathering wood, building fires, as well as cleaning up afterwards.

7) When preparing food orders, be very specific about what is wanted. Do not assume that the persons preparing your order are able to read the group's mind.

8) Plan to involve all the campers in the meal. Wood gathering, fire building, getting the food and water to the site, preparing food, cooking, serving, cleaning up (including dishes, pans, leftovers, garbage, and putting out fire) are all tasks that can be assigned to persons.

9) Spend some time after the cookout evaluating the experience—menu, procedures, quality of food, etc.

10) Remember that even though campers must eat, there is no reason to burn down the forest to cook a meal. In many areas of the country campers should carry in their "fuel." Charcoal, propane, or canned heat are adequate substitutes where wood is scarce or during times of high fire danger.

11) Food preparation may be easier when a three-point kitchen is constructed.

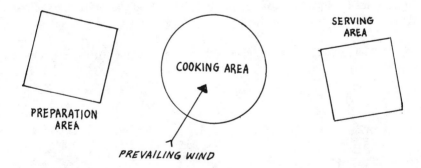

TYPES OF SIMPLE FIRES FOR COOKING

1) The hunter's fireplace is called by many the best of all. The fire is built between two green logs, but two rows of large stones make a good

substitute. The logs or stones act as supports for cooking pots, which are thus very close to the fire. Build a small fire and feed in only as needed. Coals are the best for cooking in this fireplace.

2) Trench fireplace. This is an adaptation of the hunter's fireplace. The fire is built in a trench 6 inches wide and sloping from 2 to 12 inches in depth. With a larger trench the fireplace can be lined with rocks, which, when hot, help to make a steady source of heat. This way it is unsurpassed for barbecuing on a spit built above it.

3) Bucket fires. In places where fires cannot be built on the ground (city parks, mossy woods, pavilions, etc.), an old bucket with air holes cut in the bottom and sides makes an excellent stove. This can be fed with twigs and small chunks of wood, or charcoal. It is an excellent wet weather standby, as it can be used in a tent suspended from the ridgepole.

4) Tin can fire or buddy burners. Small stoves can be made for individual cookery by utilizing number 10 cans from the kitchen. Cut an opening in the bottom of one side for putting in the sticks for firing, and at the top of the other side cut several holes for a chimney. Leave one end of the can for the top and cooking surface. The opened end sits on the ground. Use small twigs for firing. Cook bacon, pancakes, eggs, etc., directly on the top.

5) The raised hearth fireplace. Where rocks are plentiful this is a great

RESPONSIBLE WITH CREATION

"back saver" and convenience. These fireplaces can be built by stacking the rocks, or they can be made more permanent by using mud for mortar. They are exceedingly helpful in a permanent campsite where they can be used enough to make the effort necessary for their construction worthwhile. This construction makes a fine stewardship project using native materials. Another method of constructing these raised hearth fireplaces is to make a log cabin construction of green logs and fill in the middle with dirt. The fire is made on the dirt top.

6) Tin can oven. This is made from empty lard or potato chip tins. Two cans are needed. One is supported on its side on green hardwood sticks or rocks to hold it about a foot above ground. The second can is cut open with tin snips along the side seam and then halfway around the bottom. This is then supported about six inches above the first tin to reflect the heat back on the other can oven. It doesn't take much fire to keep the oven hot. Sand placed in the bottom of the oven will help prevent burning. Anything baked in an oven at home can be baked in a tin can oven with a little more watching!

METHODS OF OUTDOOR COOKING

1) Toasting on a stick (hardly challenging enough for junior highs).

Toast frankfurters, buns, toast, marshmallows, cheese sandwiches.

2) Stick broiling—over hardwood coals. Largely individualized. Peel stick and heat it before putting on food. Taste bark. If bitter do not use stick. Find another.

Pioneer drumsticks: Use hamburger; mix with egg and crushed corn-flakes, and seasoning. Squeeze in place around a stick about the size of a broomstick.

Kabobs: one-inch square of beef, one-quarter-inch thick; carrots, potatoes, and small onions alternately placed on a thin but firm green stick. Sticks trimmed to a square shape hold vegetables better. Oysters, ham, frankfurter pieces can be used instead of beef.

Steaks—fastened on twisted end of stick.

Bread twist: Use biscuit dough. Twist dough rather thinly around stick the same size as for pioneer drumstick. Turn slowly over coals. Do not let it brown until dough has expanded to twice its size on the stick.

3) One-pot meals.

Barbecued hamburger: delicious served over baked potatoes! Use hamburger, tomatoes, onions, peppers, seasoning, and barbecue sauce to taste. Fry hamburger lightly and then add all ingredients and cook together.

Stews: Use leftover meats, stew beef, or hamburger. Add potatoes and other vegetables.

Slumgullion: hamburger, one-fourth as much bacon, onions, tomatoes, one-fourth as much American cheese, seasoning. Fry diced bacon and then add onions and hamburger. Cook until meat is browned. Add tomatoes and cook fifteen minutes. Add cheese cut in small cubes. Stir till melted.

Rice and salmon: an excellent, hearty one-dish meal on a hike where food has to be carried quite a distance. Cook rice, add canned salmon, sliced green pepper, chopped celery, can of peas, and cook until vegetables are tender. Season to taste.

Chili con carne, savory beans, and chowders are other good one-pot meals.

4) Baking—in a reflector or drum oven.

Pies: Use packaged piecrust mix and native or canned berries or fruit.

Biscuits, cookies, and cake from prepared mixes.

5) Cooking directly in the coals: Be sure there are only coals; pull all flaming wood from fire.

Potatoes wrapped in mud or placed in a number 10 can with sand between the potatoes.

Roast corn in the shucks: Wet corn first.

Steaks (1-1½ inches thick) cooked right on coals—delicious for a special treat.

RESPONSIBLE WITH CREATION

Aluminum foil cooking: Double-fold all seams to prevent juices leaking.

—Potatoes wrapped in foil.

—Hamburger patty or steak with sliced potatoes, vegetables, seasonings, all wrapped and sealed together in foil.

—Tomatoes or peppers stuffed with pre-cooked meat and vegetables, seasoned, wrapped in foil.

—Fish fillet buttered and seasoned, wrapped in foil.

6) Imu cooking—cooking in pit lined with rocks, full of coals. Place food wrapped in aluminum foil or grape or sassafras leaves (or in Dutch oven) directly in coals, then cover with more coals. Cover with a damp burlap and finally cover over with 6 inches of earth to seal in heat. Allow 1½ times the regular oven cooking time.

Baked beans in Dutch ovens.

Ham wrapped in grape or sassafras leaves or aluminum foil.

Chicken wrapped in wet leaves and foil.

Fish wrapped in foil.

7) Spit cooking.

Chicken: Use barbecue sauce for basting.

Rouladen: Use beef ½ inch thick. Salt and pepper meat. Spread one side with mustard, then add minced onion. Roll around pickle. Tie with string. Spear the meat on a long green stick as you would a hot dog. Sear quickly, then broil slowly as desired.

8) Reflector roasting—roasting with heat from a reflector fire.

Planked fish on a board.

Ham or chicken suspended from wooden crane by a heavy wet cord and constantly turned.

Campers' Stew

> 3 pounds lean ground beef or 3 pounds boneless stew meat, cut in small cubes
> 2 tablespoons fat
> 4 large onions, cut in eighths
> 3 pounds potatoes, cut in cubes
> 3 pounds carrots, sliced
> 1 cup diced celery
> 2 number 2½ cans tomatoes
> salt and pepper

If you use stew meat, brown the meat and onions in fat; then add about one cup of water and cook until tender. This takes 30 minutes. Then add vegetables. If you use hamburger, brown the meat and onions; then add the vegetables, salt and pepper, and canned tomatoes. Cook until vegetables are done. Stir occasionally to keep from burning.

Barbecued Chicken

If you have large fryers, 2½ pounds or over, you may allow one-fourth of a chicken per person. If your chickens are smaller, a half fryer per person may be required. Chickens should be basted often with barbecue sauce. You will need about three cups of sauce for three chickens. Put sauce on both sides of chicken and place on grill with bony side down. Turn in about 15 minutes. Baste and cook 15 minutes. Turn and baste again. Cook about 10 minutes more. Test for doneness by turning the drumstick bone. If the bone turns in its socket easily, the chicken is done. The larger the chicken, the more time is required for cooking.

Potatoes Baked in Sand

Choose medium-sized potatoes. Wash them thoroughly and wrap them in a piece of clean paper (napkin, towel, or brown paper bag). Put a one-inch layer of wet sand in a number 10 can. Place three medium-sized or two large potatoes on the wet sand, with neither one closer than a half inch to the side of the can. Pack wet sand around the potatoes, and add a second similar layer of potatoes, covering them with wet sand. You should have a one-inch layer of sand on top. Pour a cup of water over this. *(A number 10 can should hold five or six potatoes.)*

As soon as the fire is started, set the can in the fire or in the edge of it, turning it from time to time. The potatoes will take about 45-50 minutes to cook. If the sand seems to dry out completely add more water. Set the cans aside until the rest of the dinner is prepared. The potatoes will stay hot for about half an hour. Be careful in dumping the sand, because hot sand can set leaves on fire. Unwrap the potatoes and place them on plates. You may need tongs or a fork to handle the hot potatoes.

Baked Pork Chops with Dressing

Roll pork chops in flour to which salt and pepper have been added. Put a small amount of fat in a Dutch oven, and brown the pork chops on both sides. Remove from the oven. For each six people place in the oven one package of cornbread or herb dry stuffing mix. Or you *may* want to use one package of each. Add the melted oleo as directed, reducing the amount in proportion to fat already in the oven. Make a bouillon stock by adding bouillon cubes to the required amount of water. Mix well. Put pork chops on top. Cover and bake 30-45 minutes on a grate over hot coals.

Applesauce and Gingerbread

6 cups applesauce (three number 2 cans)
1 box gingerbread mix

Heat the applesauce in a Dutch oven. Mix the gingerbread batter, following the directions on the box. When the sauce is hot, pour the batter on top, taking care not to disturb the applesauce. Cover tightly with a lid. If the lid does not fit tightly, place foil on top and then replace the lid. Simmer on hot coals for 30 minutes. Since gingerbread is to steam, avoid the temptation to take a look until the 30 minutes is up.

Cherry Pie

You will need a reflector oven or a drum oven over a medium-hot fire. One secret to cooking good pies out-of-doors is to make the crust a little shorter than for indoor oven cooking. *(This means that you use a little more fat.)* You may use a ready-mix pie crust, prepared as directed. Roll it with a juice can to fit a pie plate. Before putting the crust in a pie pan, grease the inside of the uncooked crust lightly with oleo. Now add the prepared pie filling of your choice. Make a top lattice crust by cutting the remaining dough into strips and weaving over and under to form a lattice. The pie cooks in about 30 minutes.

Mock Angel Food Cake

Roll a square of bread in sweetened condensed milk and then in coconut. Toast for a few minutes on a stick.

Some-Mores

Place a toasted marshmallow on top of a piece of graham cracker on which you have placed a square of chocolate. Cover with another graham cracker.

Baked Apples

Core apples and fill hole with butter, 1 tablespoon of water, raisins, cinnamon, and sugar. Seal in two thicknesses of foil and cook. *(Red hots may be used instead of cinnamon and sugar.)*

Hamburger Dinner

Place a hamburger patty, very thin slices of potatoes and carrots, a slice of onion, a tablespoon of butter, and seasonings on a piece of foil. Wrap and then re-wrap in a second piece of foil. Cook 10-20 minutes, turning 2 or 3 times. *Note:* Also try ham, pineapple, and sweet potatoes; or hot dogs, cheese, and bacon; or chicken pieces, onions, and potatoes.

Banana Boats

Pull back a strip of a banana peel and dig out 3 or 4 holes *(eat this)*. Fill holes with Hershey squares and marshmallows. Put outer strip back on and wrap in foil. Cook 8-10 minutes.

Hole-in-One

Cut center hole in a slice of bread *(rim of glass)*. Place bread in skillet. Drop egg in hole. Fry to taste on both sides. Can be done on hot flat granite rock.

Egg-in-Orange Shell

Supplies: 1 egg, 1 large orange, salt and pepper. Cut off top of orange. Eat orange but be careful not to tear shell. Break egg into shell. Add salt and pepper. Skewer on top of orange. Bake in coals.

Creamed Tuna

2 cans tuna	1 can cream of chicken (or
½ cup milk	mushroom) soup
2 tablespoons butter	1 onion and 1 green pepper, chopped

Saute onion and green pepper in butter until lightly brown. Add soup, milk, and tuna broken into chunks. Heat through, 10-15 minutes. Season and serve with rice, hard toast, or crackers.

Birch Tea

Supplies: 1 peck black birch twigs, 6 lemons, 1 pound sugar, large kettle, strainer, tin can pitcher, large mixing spoon.

Strip leaves from tender twigs. Cut twigs into inch pieces. Steep in hot water until water is slightly pink and flavor is strong.

7. CAMPFIRES

Small Group Pow-wows

Group living of this sort enables each member to participate in the pow-wow, or evaluation, around the evening campfire. It is here, at the close of the day, that common experiences can be discussed; that one's mistakes and successes can be recognized; that one can separate the good from the bad, the true from the false, the right from the wrong. It is here that the best insights and attitudes are developed. This is where the experiences of the day are evaluated more objectively and are seen in relation to the broader aspects of living. People are apt to feel more keenly at these times their dependence upon the world about them, and to sense with greater than usual insight their relationship to God as Creator. This sometimes becomes worship—worship at its best.[3]

A perceptive leader will sense when a group is ready for serious discussion and sharing at the deeper level and will seek to create the climate for real participation and "letting down of defenses" by questions and objective sharing of personal feelings. Sometimes a group does not seem ready to respond in discussion; at such times the singing of folk songs and hymns may prove a better way of strengthening fellowship. And sometimes the "fellowship of silence" around the embers of the fire may deepen the bonds of friendship more than anything else.

Fun Campfires

Campfires for the sheer fun of it can be had either in the small group or in larger camp groups. The latter should be more definitely planned to avoid any elements of confusion in such a large group. Fun campfires are usually made up of storytelling, games, and singing.

Storytelling

Folk tales, Indian tales, pioneer stories, and tall tales make good telling around a campfire.

Richard Chase's *Grandfather Tales, Jack Tales,* and *American Folk Tales and Songs* all have good stories in them; however, counselors should read through them first; some of the stories need minor changes in wording and a few are better not used with junior highs.

The Paul Bunyan tales, John Henry stories, and other folk tales of a particular locale are also good to tell.

Progressive tales, in which each person adds a bit to the story, and "yarn swapping" give everyone a chance to participate.

Singing

There are many excellent collections of songs for use with young people put out in pocket-sized editions. Your denomination may have one of its own. These are inexpensive songbooks so a camp can easily invest in enough for all the campers to use. Section 9 of this chapter has several suggestions for songs.

Games

Charades are lots of fun acted out at a campfire. Guessing games, riddles, relays, and rhythm games are also good. See Section 8 and the bibliography for suggestion.

Snacks

An evening campfire is always enhanced by a good snack. A group may elect to have popcorn, roast marshmallows, make hot chocolate, some-mores, or other simple items.

8. GAMES

Games, as all other camp activities, should be enjoyable but also make positive contribution to the campers' experience. Games should be chosen carefully since the effects they have on a group can vary widely. Some games can get campers quiet while others excite; some can create harmony, while others may cause discord; some can help campers have positive feelings about themselves, while others are destructive to self-image.

The games given below are examples of several types—quiet, active, nature, team, individual, etc. The camp leader will do well to refer to other resources *(including those in the bibliography)* for other usable games.

Remember—
   —Choose games with a purpose in mind.
   —Have all necessary equipment.
   —Give careful instructions.
   —Let the games be a part of the group's life, not just something to
     fill spare moments.
   —Stop the game while everyone still wants to play. That way they
     will be willing to play it again.
   —Vary the type of games played—quiet, active, brainteasers, etc.
   —Try to have games which put competition on a low key. Put indi-

viduals against themselves, not others in the group.

—Choose games at which any camper may win. Don't always favor the "athletic" type person.

—Don't run a good game into the ground.

—Have fun!

ROCKS AND LEAVES

The group is divided into two teams like "Flint" and "Oak." Each team has a leader who is the only one on the team able to pick up specimens of rocks or leaves spotted by teammates, who call him "Flint" or "Oak" as the case may be. At the end of a given time the team with the most specimens wins. This game develops observation and acquaints the group with the objects involved.

GAMES OF SMELL AND TOUCH
(good for nights or to play blindfolded during the day)

Identify objects by smell. Good items are: pine, balsam, cedar, sassafras, mint, birch, wintergreen, pennyroyal, skunk cabbage, onion, sarsaparilla, apple, orange, tomato, humus.

Identify objects by touch. Good items are: bark, leaves, fruits, vegetables, evergreens, some seeds, nuts, flowers, feathers, shells, and soils.

NATURE RELAYS

Have at opposite end of room several piles of scrambled natural objects. The leader of each relay team is given a list with as many items on it as there are players in line. At a signal, leader looks at first item on list, gives list to second player, and then goes to pile to get first object on list. When first returns with correct object, second may go to claim second item on list, and so on down the line.

RHYTHM

Number the players consecutively around the circle. The game is played to a clapping, finger-snapping rhythm of four counts. On the first and second beats let players slap their legs with both hands; on the third beat, let them snap their right-hand fingers; on the fourth beat, their left-hand fingers. Number one begins the game by starting the rhythm. On the snap of the right hand the player calls his/her number and on the snap of the left hand the number of another person. The person whose number is called must respond in rhythm by repeating his/her number on the next snap of the right hand and calling another number on the snap of the left hand. Any person who fails to respond in rhythm, goes to the end of the circle and becomes the last number. All those below the miss then move up one number to fill the vacancy. The object of the game is to become number one. Number one starts the rhythm again after each miss.

BUZZ OR BUZZ-FIZZ

This is a counting game. A player starts the game by saying "one," and the count goes around the circle clockwise. Instead of saying "seven" or any number containing seven or a multiple of seven, the player must respond with "buzz," and the next player goes on with the count. Thus the counting would be "Six, *buzz,* eight...thirteen, *buzz,* fifteen, sixteen, *buzz,* eighteen...." Penalty for failure to buzz at the proper time is to pay a forfeit or drop out of the game. "Fizz" is a variation which is added when the group becomes good at buzzing. "Fizz" is said instead of five or multiples of five. Still another variation is to reverse the direction of counting at each buzz or fizz.

NATURE SCAVENGER HUNT

Divide the group into pairs and give each pair an identical list of items to be found in nature. First pair returning with a correct and complete list wins. *Stress conservation practices.* Some suggested items to include on the list are:

Flower of Queen Anne's lace	Hickory nut
Snail	Oak leaf with bristles
Ant	Maple leaf
Grass gone to seed	Piece of limestone
Three shapes of leaves from the same tree	Bird's feather
Fungus	Moth
Acorn	

9. SONGS AND MUSIC

Music is a wonderful and lovely gift of God. Next to theology, music is God's finest gift to man. It is a soothing and refreshing balm for every troubled soul; it dispels gloom and drives away our worries and makes man cheerful and contented.

—Martin Luther

Singing is an important part of any group's experience at camp. Too many camp leaders fail to take advantage of what singing can do for a group, saying that they cannot sing well enough to lead. It is unfortunate that such leaders deprive campers of such a joyous part of camp life. One does not have to know how to sing in order to help campers enjoy singing. Singing is a natural expression, especially when campers are happy. Every camper should return home at the end of camp session having learned some new and good songs.

Most singing in your small group will be spontaneous, as campers sit around a campfire, rest on a hike, or are busy doing other things. A leader who plans well will be prepared to guide a group in their choice of songs so that they do not choose songs that make fun of persons or become monotonous through senseless repetition. There will be other times *(especially during worship or study)* when the leader will want to teach the group new songs. It is not necessary to have songbooks, but it is helpful to have the words printed on individual sheets or on a large poster board. Persons learn songs through repetition. When teaching a song plan on using it several times during the session.

Remember that songs can set the mood of a group. When a group is loud around a campfire, begin singing some loud fun songs and begin to gradually tone them down until the desired mood is reached.

There are several small pocket-sized songbooks on the market which your camp may own. If they are available, it would be good to have them in the leaders' resource kit.

HIKING SONGS

We're Marching to Pretoria
We're on the Upward Trail
The Happy Wanderer
Swinging Along

Make New Friends
Holla Hi, Holla Ho
Sing Your Way Home
Ol' Texas

FUN SONGS

If You're Happy
Sarasponda
Music Alone Shall Live
In a Cabin
Do-Re-Mi
Alouette
Vive l-Amour
Cuckoo
Let Us Sing Together
I Love the Mountains
Toviska
Whippoorwill

TRADITIONAL FOLK SONGS

Swing Low Sweet Chariot
Jacob's Ladder
Old Smoky
Go Tell It on the Mountain
Kookaburra
The Ash Grove
Home on the Range
Barbara Allen
Down in the Valley
King of Kings
Go Tell Aunt Rhody

MODERN FOLK SONGS

Lord of the Dance
Michael Row Your Boat
Joy Is Like the Rain
Where Have All the Flowers Gone
Blowing in the Wind
If I Had a Hammer
Five Hundred Miles
This Land Is Your Land
They'll Know We Are Christians
He's Got the Whole World

QUIET SONGS

Spirit of the Living God
Kum Ba Yah
Lonesome Valley

Tallis' Canon
Evening Skies
Peace Like a River
Each Campfire Lights Anew
Tell Me Why

RELIGIOUS SONGS

This Is My Father's World
Amazing Grace
Let Us Break Bread Together
Day Is Dying
O Young and Fearless Prophet
Dakota Hymn
Now the Day Is Over
Our Father
For the Beauty of the Earth

10. RAINY DAY ACTIVITIES

For the most part, camping activities are carried on as usual even if it is raining. Additional tarps and scrap canvas can be stretched to provide more protection at the campsite so that a group can continue to cook or build there. Sometimes, if it is storming too hard, a group could do as one group did, and cook their food over fires made in old buckets with holes punched in the bottom of them and suspended by wire from the ridgepoles of their shelter. Working together to overcome difficulties binds a group more closely and they have a lot of fun in the process. Campers enjoy being ingenious.

Rainy days are ideal times to work on craft projects from natural materials. These materials may have been gathered earlier or they could be gathered on a rain hike: wood for whittling and carving, vines, reeds and grasses for weaving, and other items that can be used.

There are unique opportunities afforded by rainy days. Hikes in the rain can be a lot of fun, provided campers are dressed properly and get back to their shelters to change clothes before they get too wet or chilled. In the rain, campers can see what water erosion can do when it is not controlled and they may be moved to undertake a service project to help control erosion, like building check dams or terraces, or transplanting seedlings and sod. Sometimes storms wash up driftwood and other interesting things along the shore. Scavenger hunts for things hard to find in the rain are fun—a dry leaf, a butterfly, a feather, etc. Or test a group's campcraft skill by building a fire in the rain, finding dry wood without raiding the woodpile. If the weather is warm and it is not during an electrical storm, take a swim or build a dam in a brook. Try having a boat race floating leaf or bark boats—it's silly but fun!

Other groups have used rainy days for telling stories, learning new songs, and taking more time in discussion and Bible study. Rainy days provide time for delving into resource books for ideas and information, for sketching and writing, and for working out dramas.

The attitude of the counselor toward the rain will influence the attitudes of the campers. The counselor may assure the group that the rain affords opportunities to do some things that could not be done in dry weather. Such a positive approach will help develop the proper appreciation for the rain.

> "All sunshine and no rain
> doth a desert make."

Below are listed several activities which take place during a rain and which actually use the rain as a program resource. *(By the way, did you list weather as a possible resource for your use when you were listing possible resources?)*

What Can I Do with a Small Group *in* the Rain *with* the Rain?

1. Study cloud formation.
2. Study lightning.
3. Study wind velocity.
4. Study purity and quality of rainwater.
5. Study water temperature.
6. Study erosion: how, where, why, and how to prevent and correct it.
7. Study absorption/saturation rates of water in various types of soil.
8. Study how moisture affects: how sound travels, how smoke rises, a barometer, a hydrometer, canvas shelters (expansion and contraction).
9. Study causes of rain and water cycle.
10. Study benefits of rain.
11. Study effects of too much rain.
12. Study effects of rain on: insects (worms), various types of plants, various types of animals, various types of ground cover.
13. Measure rainfall.
14. Forecast future weather. When will rain stop?
15. Hunt for a rainbow and discuss why if you find one.

16. Discuss precautions to take during rain.
17. Participate in an erosion control project.
18. Discuss land use as it relates to flooding.
19. Have a hike.
20. Discuss difference between "waterproof" and "water repellent."

11. SCRIPTURE PASSAGES RELATED
TO THE OUTDOORS

Exodus 3:1-12—Moses was in the wilderness keeping sheep when God spoke to him out of the burning bush.

Exodus 19:16—20:17—God revealed to Moses the commandments for people living together in their camp community.

1 Kings 19:1-18—God spoke to a disillusioned Elijah in the still, small voice in the wilderness.

Psalms 8, 23, 91, 104, 121—David came to know and trust God during his long days and nights out in the wilderness tending his sheep.

Amos 1:1 and 7:14-15—God's will was revealed for Israel to Amos during the long days and nights he spent as a shepherd of Tekoa.

Jesus spent much of his life in the out-of-doors:

Matthew 3:13—4:11—His baptism and temptation experiences took place outdoors.

Matthew 14:23 and Luke 6:12—He often spent the night alone in prayer on a hillside.

Matthew 5:1-20 and Luke 5:1-11—He often taught outdoors.

Matthew 8:23-27—He trusted God in a storm.

His teaching used illustrations taken from the outdoors:

Matthew 6:25-34—God's care for the created things, the birds, and the flowers.

Matthew 13:1-9, 18-23—The sower.

Matthew 13:24-30, 36-43—The good seed and the bad seed.

Matthew 13:31-32—The mustard seed.

Matthew 16:1-3 and Luke 12:54-56—Knowing the signs of the sky.

Mark 4:26-29—God makes seeds to grow.

Luke 6:43-45—A good tree bears good fruit.

Luke 13:6-9—The fig tree.

Luke 15:3-7—The lost sheep.

RESPONSIBLE WITH CREATION

12. BIBLIOGRAPHY

Many of the resources listed are out of print but may be available in your local, camp, or church library.

Camp Administration and Philosophy

Camp, the Child's World. Martinsville, Indiana: American Camping Association, 1962.

Carlson, Reynold. *The Values of Camping.* American Camping Association, 1975.

Creative Church Camping. Philadelphia: Lutheran Church Press, 1971.

Davis, Robert P. *Church Camping.* Richmond, Virginia: John Knox Press, 1969.

Elder, Frederick. *Crisis in Eden: A Religious Study of Man and Environment.* Nashville: Abingdon Press, 1970.

Gabel, Peter S. *Camping Creates Community.* American Camping Association, 1971.

Harper, Bud. *Growing Inside, Outside.* The United Church of Canada, Board of Christian Education, 1969.

Johnson, C. Walton. *The Unique Mission of the Summer Camp.* American Camping Association, 1973.

Johnson, Ronald K. *Planning Outdoor Christian Education.* Philadelphia: United Church Press, 1972.

Rodney, Lynn S., & Ford, Phyllis M. *Camp Administration.* New York: John Wiley & Sons, 1971.

Webb, Kenneth. *Camping for American Youth.* American Camping Association, 1962.

Webb. *Summer Camps: Security in the Midst of Change.* A.C.A., 1968.

Westerhoff, John H., III. *How Can We Teach Values?* Philadelphia: United Church Press, 1969.

Witt, Ted R. *Toward Excellence in Church Camping.* Nashville: Discipleship Resources, 1974.

Nature and Ecology Activities and Source Books

Alexander, Taylor R., & Fichter, George S. *Ecology* (Golden Science Guide Series). New York: Golden Press, 1973.

Bachert, Russell E. *Eco-Sketch: Ideas for Environmental Education.* American Camping Association, 1976.

Brown, Vinson. *Knowing the Outdoors in the Dark.* New York: Macmillan, 1973.

Brown. *Reading the Woods.* Macmillan, 1973.

Cassell, Sylvia. *Nature Games and Activities.* New York: Harper & Row, 1956.

Frankel, Lillian, & Frankel, Godfrey. *101 Best Nature Games and Projects.* New York: Gramercy Publishing Co., 1959.

Gardner, John F. *A Book of Nature Activities.* Danville, Illinois: Interstate, 1967.

Golden Nature Guide Series. New York: Golden Press.

Titles available include:

Birds	Butterflies & Moths
Fishes	Flowers
Fossils	Game Birds
Geology	Insect Pests
Insects	Mammals
Nonflowering Plants	Pond Life
Reptiles & Amphibians	Rocks & Minerals
Spiders & Their Kin	Stars
Trees	Weather
Weeds	Zoology

Headstrom, Richard. *Adventures with a Hand Lens.* Philadelphia: J. B. Lippincott, 1962.

Hillcourt, William. *New Field Book of Nature Activities and Hobbies.* New York: Putnam, 1978.

Hillcourt. *Outdoor Things to Do.* New York: Golden Press, 1975.

Hirsch, S. Carl. *The Living Community.* New York: The Viking Press, 1966.

Leopold, Aldo. *Sand County Almanac & Sketches Here & There.* New York: Oxford University Press, 1949.

Nickelsburg, Janet. *Field Trips: Ecology for Youth Leaders.* Minneapolis: Burgess Publishing Co., 1966.

OBIS-ACA Camp Activity Kit (Outdoor Biology Instructional Strategies). American Camping Association, 1976.

Paetkau, Paul. *God, Man, Land.* Newton, Kansas: Faith & Life Press, 1978.

Peterson, Roger Torv. ed. *Field Guide Series.* Boston: Houghton Mifflin.

Titles include:

Animal Tracks	Mammals
Birds	Reptiles & Amphibians
Butterflies	Rocks & Minerals
Edible Wild Plants	Trees & Shrubs
Ferns	Western Birds
Insects	Wild Flowers

Storer, John H. *The Web of Life.* New York: New American Library, 1972.

Van Der Smissen, Betty, et al. *A Leader's Guide to Nature-Oriented Activities,* 2nd ed. Ames, Iowa: Iowa State University Press, 1968.

Van Matre, Steve. *Acclimatization.* American Camping Association, 1972.

Van Matre. *Acclimatizing.* A.C.A., 1974.

Group Activities: Stories, Games, Songs

Berger, H. Jean. *Program Activities for Camps.* Minneapolis: Burgess Publishing Co., 1969.

Buskin, David. *Outdoor Games.* New York: Lion Press, 1966.

RESPONSIBLE WITH CREATION

Camp Program Ideas. Recreation Department, San Diego State University, 1977.

Chase, Richard. *American Folk Tales & Songs.* New York: Dover Pubns., 1971.

Chase. *Grandfather Tales.* Boston: Houghton Mifflin, 1948.

Chase. *Jack Tales.* Houghton Mifflin, 1943.

Eisenberg, Helen, & Eisenberg, Larry. *The Handbook of Skits and Stunts.* New York: Association Press, 1953.

Fluegelman, Andrew, ed. *The New Games Book.* New York: Doubleday, 1976.

Frost, Robert. *You Come Too.* New York: Holt, Rinehart & Winston, 1959.

Holderness, Ginny Ward. *The Exuberant Years: A Guide for Junior High Leaders.* Atlanta: John Knox Press, 1976.

Kuntz, Bob. *Stories You Can Tell.* Nashville: Discipleship Resources, 1977.

Mackay, Joy. *Raindrops Keep Falling on My Tent.* Wheaton, Illinois: Victor Books, 1972.

Musselman, Virginia W. *Learning About Nature Through Games.* Harrisburg, Pennsylvania: The Stackpole Co., 1967.

Simley, Anne. *Folk Tales to Tell or Read Aloud.* Burgess, 1963.

Simon, Sidney B. *Meeting Yourself Halfway.* Niles, Illinois: Argus Communications, 1974.

Thurston, LaRue A. *Good Times Around the Campfire.* Association Press, 1967.

Tobitt, Janet. *Counselor's Guide to Camp Singing.* American Camping Association, 1971.

Wigginton, Eliot. *The Foxfire Book.* Doubleday, 1975. (Now 4 volumes.)

Understanding Junior Highs

Browning, Robert L. *Communicating with Junior Highs.* Nashville: Graded Press, 1968.

Johnson, Eric W. *How to Live Through Junior High School.* Philadelphia: J. B. Lippincott, 1975.

Van Krevelen, Alice. *Children in Groups: Psychology and the Summer Camp.* Belmont, California: Wadsworth Publishing Co., 1972.

Counseling Skills

Beker, Jerry. *Training Camp Counselors in Human Relations.* New York: Association Press, 1962.

Bloom, Joel W. *Camper Guidance in the Routines of Daily Living.* American Camping Association, 1965.

Camper Guidance: A Basic Handbook for Counselors. A.C.A., 1961.

Hammett, Catherine T. *A Camp Director Trains His Own Staff.* A.C.A., 1947.

Ledlie, John A., & Holbein, F. W. *Camp Counselor's Manual.* Association Press, 1969.

Mitchell, Viola, et al. *Camp Counseling.* Philadelphia: W. B. Saunders, 1977.

Worship Resources

Bays, Alice. *Worship Services for Teen-agers.* Nashville: Abingdon Press, 1958.

Bowman, Clarice. *Spiritual Values in Ca* ——
1954.

Bowman. *Worship Ways for Camp.* As——

MacInnes, Gordon A. *A Guide to* ——
delphia: The Westminster Press,

Pease, Dorothy Wells. *Meditation*

Schroeder, Ruth. *Youth Progra*

Taylor, Wesley D. *Lifesprin*
Ministry. Salem, Oregon:

Crafts and Campcraft

Bale, Robert O. *Creative*
1959.

Bale. *Outdoor Living.* Burgess, 1961.

Bale. *What on Earth.* American Camping As——

Hammett, Catherine T. *Your Own Book of Campcra*
1950.

Hawkinson, John. *Collect, Print, and Paint from Nature.* Chic——
Albert & Co., 1963.

Jaeger, Ellsworth. *Nature Crafts.* New York: Macmillan, 1950.

Kinser, Charleen. *Outdoor Art for Kids.* Chicago: Follett Publishing Co., 1975.

Musselman, Virginia W. *Learning About Nature Through Crafts.* Harrisburg, Pennsylvania: The Stackpole Company, 1969.

Stinson, Thelma. *Native 'N' Creative.* Nashville: Methodist Board of Education, 1957.

Thomas, Dian. *Roughing It Easy: A Unique Ideabook for Camping & Cooking.* Provo, Utah: Brigham Young University Press, 1974.

Notes

1. Lynn and Campbell Loughmiller, *Camping and Christian Growth* (Nashville: Abingdon Press, 1953).

2. Reprinted by permission from *A Leader's Guide to Nature-Oriented Activities* by Betty van der Smissen and Oswald Goering, Third Edition, © 1977 by The Iowa State University Press, Ames, Iowa 50010.

3. Adapted from *Camping and Christian Growth* by Loughmiller, p. 40.

RESPONSIBLE WITH CREATION